A Place in My Heart

A Place in My Heart

ANUPAMA CHOPRA

VINTAGE

An imprint of Penguin Random House

VINTAGE

USA | Canada | UK | Ireland | Australia
New Zealand | India | South Africa | China

Vintage is part of the Penguin Random House group of companies
whose addresses can be found at global.penguinrandomhouse.com

Published by Penguin Random House India Pvt. Ltd
4th Floor, Capital Tower 1, MG Road,
Gurugram 122 002, Haryana, India

Penguin
Random House
India

First published in Vintage by Penguin Random House India 2021

10 9 8 7 6 5 4 3 2 1

The views and opinions expressed in the book are those of the author only and do not
reflect or represent the views and opinions held by any other person. This book is based
on a variety of sources including interviews and interactions conducted by the author
with the persons mentioned in the manuscript. It reflects the author's own understanding
and conception of such materials and/or can be verified by research. The objective of this
book is not to hurt any sentiments or be biased in favour of or against any particular
person, industry, region, caste, society, gender, creed, nation or religion.

ISBN 9780670094998

Typeset in Adobe Caslon Pro by Manipal Technologies Limited, Manipal
Printed at Thomson Press India Ltd, New Delhi

www.penguin.co.in

To my parents—Navin and Kamna Chandra—who were bewildered by my career choice ('Bollywood journalist, are you sure?') but supported every decision I made, including marrying into the mob. Thank you.

Contents

Introduction   ix

1. Sholay   1
2. Amitabh Bachchan   5
3. The Lunchbox   10
4. Tungrus   14
5. Angamaly Diaries   17
6. Chak De! India   20
7. Chashme Buddoor   25
8. Dil Chahta Hai   29
9. Don   33
10. Duniya Na Mane   37
11. Hazaaron Khwaishein Aisi   40
12. Hum Dil De Chuke Sanam   44
13. In Which Annie Gives It Those Ones   48
14. Kabhi Kabhie   52
15. Kal Ho Naa Ho   57
16. Karan Johar   61
17. Karz   65
18. Kumbalangi Nights   69
19. LSD: Love, Sex Aur Dhokha   72
20. Luck by Chance   76

21. Jio MAMI Mumbai Film Festival   80
22. Maqbool   85
23. Monsoon Wedding   89
24. Mughal-e-Azam   93
25. Nayakan   97
26. Priyanka Chopra Jonas   101
27. Rangeela   106
28. Satya   110
29. Super Deluxe   115
30. The Cinema Travellers   118
31. Theatres   121
32. Supermen of Malegaon   125
33. Kabhi Khushi Kabhie Gham . . .   128
34. Kalyug   132
35. C/o Kancharapalem   136
36. Loins of Punjab Presents   139
37. Masoom   143
38. Mirch Masala   147
39. Sairat   151
40. The Namesake   156
41. Udaan   160
42. Vada Chennai   164
43. Aaranya Kaandam   168
44. Bandit Queen   173
45. Celluloid Man   178
46. Chalti Ka Naam Gaadi   182
47. Daayraa   186
48. Diljit Dosanjh   190
49. Guide   194
50. Aditya Chopra   198
51. The Cannes Film Festival   202

Acknowledgements   207
References   209

Introduction

Sometime in the summer of 1989, I fell in love with Bollywood. That term hadn't yet become a moniker for the Hindi film industry. Neither was it an attention-grabbing, instantly recognizable global brand. If anything, Bollywood stood for a chaotic, loosely-cobbled-together world that, more than anything, resembled the Wild West. It was a world brimming with gaudy, larger-than-life personalities who made, mostly, gaudy, larger-than-life films. Contracts were as rare as bound scripts. The money sometimes came with shady strings attached. There was billowing colour, flashes of artistry and more than a touch of recklessness—you heard of producers who had sold their homes to make movies, and actors who flitted from one set to another like bees pollinating flowers. Bollywood was an ecosystem fuelled by luck and money, gambling and glamour. In short, it was irresistible.

My love affair expanded and endured. After Hindi cinema, I became passionate about Hollywood and world cinema. Film festivals taught me new ways of seeing. I embraced not just the movies but the people who made them. I came to understand the adrenaline highs of the business and the piercing loneliness of failure. I came to relish not just the beauty and magic of the art form but everything that came with it, from the crazy deals (I've seen payments made with suitcases of cash) to the constantly shifting power structure (each Friday decides your fate afresh), to the ugly, desperate pursuit for success, which remains elusive, treacherous and uniquely lonely. Inevitably, I married into the mob.

Over the years, films, artists, events, spaces continued to fire my grand passion and lodge themselves deep in me. This book is a journey through some of these. *A Place in My Heart* is about a life defined by cinema. I want to share with you everything in entertainment that has, as Marie Kondo would put it, 'sparked joy' in me. I hope that it does the same for you.

1

Sholay

Sholay is my first movie memory. I was eight years old when it released in 1975. I remember watching the film in a theatre and being terrified, not just of Gabbar Singh but also of that screeching, wailing background score that kicked in every time he appeared—there was a haunting menace to it.

As I got older, I kept revisiting the film and it soon became a favourite. I started to see the masterful storytelling, the layers in its characters (even the minor ones like the '*Angrezon ke zamane ke* jailer' and Soorma Bhopali), the uniqueness of the setting (the rugged badlands of Ramgarh) and the astute comedy (the *tanki* scene is a classic but even Jai's snarky asides to Basanti are gold). *Sholay* is one of the finest examples of the traditional Hindi film form, which seamlessly blends genres. As Veeru so memorably put it, '*Iss* story *mein* emotion *hai*, drama *hai*, tragedy *hai*.'

It is almost impossible for a viewer today to comprehend the seismic impact of the film when it first came out. It ran in Mumbai's Minerva theatre for five years. Even in its 240th week, it was houseful. The film's box-office collections—it grossed approximately Rs 35 crore in that first run—remained unmatched for nineteen years, till *Hum Aapke Hain Koun . . !* released in 1994. The film's cultural influence was even farther-reaching. So much of the dialogue has passed into colloquial usage that, even taken out of context, phrases like '*Bahut yaarana hai*' or '*Kitne aadmi the?*' or '*Arre o Sambha*' still carry a world of meaning. More than thirty years after its release, characters and lines from *Sholay* were being used to sell products and as comedic fodder in skits and in other films. In *Mere Brother Ki Dulhan*, released in 2011, Katrina Kaif re-enacts the *tanki* scene. Her character Dimple prefaces the performance with: '*Main batati hoon* film *kya hoti hai,* dialogue *kya hotein hai,* acting *kya hoti hai*'.

That is exactly what *Sholay* is: a masterclass in cinema. Other films from the 1970s might seem shoddy and dated now, but *Sholay* has aged like a bottle of Château Lafite Rothschild. It still hits all the right notes. As Shekhar Kapur so rightly put it: 'There has never been a more defining film on the Indian screen. Indian film history can be divided into *Sholay* BC and *Sholay* AD.'

Sholay started as a four-line story, which writers Javed Akhtar and Salim Khan took a mere fifteen days to develop into an outline. The set-up isn't startlingly original: the prime mover of the story is Thakur Baldev Singh, who hires two petty thieves, Veeru and Jai, to hunt down a brutal dacoit named Gabbar Singh who has massacred Thakur's family. The writers, who then wrote under the moniker of Salim-Javed, were inspired by films like *Butch Cassidy and the Sundance Kid*, Sergio Leone's Spaghetti Westerns and Akira Kurosawa's *Seven Samurai*, arguably the mother of all mercenary movies. *Sholay* also has echoes of Raj Khosla's 1971 hit, *Mera Gaon Mera Desh*, and of the successful B-grade Indian Western,

Khote Sikkay. But Salim-Javed and director Ramesh Sippy were able to take this familiar genre material and refashion it into something that proved to be innovative and enduring—the denim outfits, the horses, the guns and the steam engines give the film an ageless quality.

Sholay is a rare film that can be watched any number of times—I still get goosebumps when Thakur walks into his home with gifts for his family, only to see a row of bodies in shrouds. I still get teary when, after Jai's death, the widow Radha—who had perhaps imagined a future of love and laughter with him—shuts the window of her room, as though shutting out life itself. The writing, the characters, the performances, even the humour (think of Jai sarcastically asking, '*Tumhara naam kya hai, Basanti?*') still hold. The beats of the narrative, which moves from terrifying violence to comedy, song and dance, and drama, still exert a formidable grip.

Sholay changed the lives of everyone connected to it—even the peripheral characters. The late Mac Mohan played Gabbar Singh's henchman, Sambha. Sambha has only one line in the film—when Gabbar asks what reward the government has announced for capturing him, Sambha replies: '*Poore pachaas hazaar*'. But Mac Mohan said that the popularity of the film made him lose his identity. He told me that when people approached him for an autograph, they looked bewildered when he signed Mac Mohan because they thought his name was Sambha!

Another minor player, Viju Khote, was immortalized as Kaalia, a henchman whom Gabbar shoots after famously asking: '*Tera kya hoga, Kaalia?*' Until his death in 2019, Viju had people addressing him by the character's name. He told me that when people on the street sometimes recognized him and shouted 'Kaalia!', his son would get angry, but then Viju would explain: 'We are eating our bread and butter because of that.'

I interviewed these actors for a book I wrote on the film. In 2000, *Sholay* celebrated its twenty-fifth anniversary. Ramesh Sippy's children—Rohan, Sheena and Sonya—wanted to mark the occasion with a book that chronicled the struggle and passion that went into making the film. Ramesh and his crew had defied traditional industry wisdom and worked against gargantuan odds. They had strived for nearly two years, over 450 shifts, to create a singular work of art. Sometime in 1999, I was invited to trace the story of the making of the film. I spent months doing research, interviewing the principal cast and crew, and trying to shape the material into a narrative that would be at least a fraction as compelling as the film itself. I was deathly afraid of doing something that *Sholay* never does—boring the audience.

Sholay: The Making of a Classic was published in 2000. The following year, it won the National Award for Best Book on Cinema. As I went up on stage to accept the award from President K.R. Narayanan, I understood that the cinema gods were still smiling down on the film. My book begins with a tarot card reader named Dolores Pereira who, sometime in 1974, had met Ramesh Sippy and Amjad Khan in Bangalore and predicted that *Sholay* would run for many years. Dolores was right about that, but I don't think even she could have imagined that the writer of a book on the film would also be rewarded with such a high honour.

Over the decades, I've fallen in love with hundreds of movies. But *Sholay* will always be special. You can watch the film on YouTube.* If you haven't seen it, you really should. And if you have, well, then you know what I'm talking about.

---

* Availability of films might change over time.

2

Amitabh Bachchan

'This is Amitabh,' he said, as though that baritone could belong to anyone else. It was my first encounter with the actor. We were speaking on the phone, sometime in 1995. The great American photographer Mary Ellen Mark had been commissioned by the film magazine *Premiere* to do a photo shoot with leading actors in the Hindi film industry. I was an editorial assistant, helping to line up the talent. On the wish list was the leading man who had defined Hindi cinema for decades.

These were pre-cell phone days. I left messages with his secretary, which is what talent managers were called then. A few days later, he called back. I was a newbie but I had a master's degree in journalism from Northwestern University. I considered myself too professional and too inherently cool to be swayed by Bollywood stardom. And yet, something about his voice was so commanding that I had to sit down to have the conversation. He was exceedingly polite. I can't remember why, but he declined to do the shoot.

Amitabh Bachchan is India's most enduring superstar. He has been a part of our collective psyche for more than fifty years. He cuts a colossus-like figure, towering over films, television, commercials, the press and even social media, with millions of followers across platforms. When an actor has lasted that long, he becomes a human Rorschach test, signifying different things to different people. Your take and your degree of attachment to Mr Bachchan (I wouldn't dare address him as anything but that or 'Sir') depend on your vintage, gender, taste.

For those of us who came of age in the 1980s and 1990s, he was, as *India Today* magazine dubbed him, a one-man industry. So outsized and dazzling that we barely noticed anything else in the frame.

We grew up on the singular heroism of Mr Bachchan. Some of my favourite Hindi films are still the ones from the 1970s that first established him as a star. The Angry Young Man, created by the brilliant Salim-Javed in the early '70s, was an archetype that shaped the narrative in mainstream Hindi cinema for two decades. In films like *Zanjeer*, *Deewaar*, *Sholay* and *Trishul*, Mr Bachchan delivered performances that still crackle with frisson.

Unlike the other leading men of the time, he wasn't handsome in that fair-skin, '*khaate-peete-ghar-ka*' way. Instead, he was lean and gangly. In these films, there was something bruised and brooding about him. When we first met these characters, we instinctively understood that they had already survived some personal hell.

Look at Vijay's furious expression in *Zanjeer*, when he kicks the chair in the police station and tells Sher Khan (played by a terrific Pran), '*Jab tak baithne ko na kaha jaaye, sharafat se khade raho. Yeh police station hai, tumhare baap ka ghar nahi.*' Or the hurt and desperation in his voice, when, as the angst-ridden criminal Vijay in *Deewaar*, he walks into a temple for the first time in his life and begs God to punish him but save his dying mother. Or that defiant dignity with which, when money is flung at him in the same film, he says, '*Main aaj bhi phenke hue paise nahi uthata.*'

But Mr Bachchan's brilliance is that his artistry is, to steal a phrase from Shakespeare, one of 'infinite variety'. So the same actor could, in the same film, be equally effective as the superbly suave Don, who declares with effortless cool: '*Don ko pakadna mushkil hi nahi, namumkin hai*', and the country bumpkin Vijay, the '*Ganga-kinare wala chhora*' who explodes with joy when he can finally stop pretending to be the smooth criminal Don and instead drink *bhang* and chew on some '*paan Banaraswala*'. The song has millions of views on YouTube because Mr Bachchan's effervescence is contagious. He makes you want to dance with that same abandon.

Mr Bachchan could also be, with equal ease, the liquor dealer Anthony in Manmohan Desai's classic *Amar Akbar Anthony*, creating one of Hindi cinema's most iconic drunk scenes; and the poet Amit in Yash Chopra's *Kabhi Kabhie*, the '*pal do pal ka shayar*' who voluntarily gives up the woman he loves but then spends a lifetime nursing the scars of his failed love story.

Ironically, the actor who could effortlessly juggle drama, romance, music, comedy and tragedy ended up being straitjacketed by his own stardom. Mr Bachchan became so successful that filmmakers stopped being inventive with him. Through the '80s especially, he seemed trapped, playing watered-down versions of roles he had done before.

Over the decades, Mr Bachchan's gargantuan stardom has waxed and waned.

A detour into politics in the mid-'80s and a series of mediocre comeback films after his sabbatical in the mid-'90s proved to be disastrous. But his fundamental ability to connect with the audience remained intact. Which is why his hold over our imaginations, reignited by the television show *Kaun Banega Crorepati* (*KBC*, launched in 2000), hasn't faltered despite the generations of new actors who came after, including the Khan trinity: Salman, Shah Rukh and Aamir.

From the anti-establishment crusader, he evolved into the nation's favourite patriarch. On *KBC*, there was something reassuring about his dignified presence in our homes every night. With his amiable manner, impeccable Hindi and sartorial elegance, he elevated not just the game show format but Indian television as a whole. He was the first A-list star to make this crossover and do it in a way that amplified rather than downsized his image.

It's hard to describe what Mr Bachchan means to people. I remember one of my earliest assignments as a cub reporter for *Movie* magazine. We used to go studio-hopping and try and get interviews with stars who happened to be shooting on the day. One day, I walked into the Filmistan studio and asked a lightman, '*Aaj kaun aaya hai?*' He simply said, '*Bhagwan.*' Bachchan was in the building (I didn't get the interview). And yet, despite this pedestal that we have placed him on, his humility is so unshakeable that it's exasperating. Through the years, we've done several interviews, and each time I've asked about his stardom, he's dismissed it as a 'media-made' construct. He simply refuses to acknowledge his own myth.

And yet, it is this very myth that has made him such an effective voice on everything from polio vaccination and anti-tuberculosis drives to climate change. Generations of Indians have been gently, with a nudge and a wink, reminded to be healthier, kinder, better.

What helps to make the mythification more palatable is his wicked sense of humour. I recall an interview we did for the American trade magazine *Variety*. He had recently started his blog and was taking me through a typical day in his life, which included exercising at dawn, shooting through the day and writing for the blog around midnight. I asked, 'When do you sleep?' He replied with a straight face, 'During interviews.' These zingers aren't accompanied by any change in expression. He keeps a straight face but you can see the mischief in his eyes.

One of Mr Bachchan's long-standing complaints about me has been my faulty Hindi. Like him, I'm from Uttar Pradesh, and he has advised me repeatedly to sharpen my mother tongue. He's even reminded me on Twitter. On 31 December 2017, I posted my New Year resolutions for 2018. He promptly posted a response to my post, saying, 'Why wait for New Year to do all this . . . you should do it everyday! . . . errm . . . one resolution missing . . . learn to speak Hindi, if you are reviewing Hindi cinema.' It was like being scolded in public by an elder in the family!

Mr Bachchan's films have shaped my understanding and expectations of cinema. His performances, and the dexterity and conviction with which he played even the most outlandish roles, nurtured in me a life-long love of Hindi films. This is an actor who, in *Amar Akbar Anthony*, could step out of a giant egg, wearing a top hat, tailcoat and monocle, blabbering gibberish, and create not just delightful comedy but also a new expression of love. There aren't too many actors who could do that.

My favourite Mr Bachchan memory, though, is from a poetry-reading session on a terrace. There were few people present. He read his father Harivansh Rai Bachchan's classic, *Madhushala*, patiently stopping to explain the lines that he knew I wouldn't understand. The wisdom and warmth in his voice was magic. Like the exquisite poetry he was reciting, Mr Bachchan is one for the ages. His first name means everlasting light—and what could be more fitting?

3

The Lunchbox

'Kabhi kabhi galat train *bhi sahi jagah pahucha deti hai.'*

Trains play a lead role in Ritesh Batra's 2013 film, *The Lunchbox*. The film opens with a wide shot of the Mumbai locals, which ferry millions across the city daily. These trains, the beating heart of a bustling city, also carry back and forth the famous *dabbawallas*, who transport hot lunches from homes to offices. Established in 1890, this army of over 5,000 men, dressed in white and wearing traditional Gandhi caps, delivers meals to more than 2,00,000 people daily. Their system is so intricate and accurate that it's been written about in the *New York Times* and the *Harvard Business Review*. Their error ratio is 1 in 6 million. *The Lunchbox* is the story of what happens when that one *dabba* ends up at the wrong address.

'Only connect . . .' E.M. Forster wrote as the epigraph to his 1910 novel, *Howards End*. *The Lunchbox* is about a connection that two people make through food and then through handwritten letters. This is an epistolary romance in a sense, but the word 'romance' burdens the delicacy of the relationship between Ila and Saajan. She's a housewife, trapped in a souring marriage (she suspects her husband is having an affair—he barely notices her but is quick to criticize the lunches she sends him) and stifling domesticity (her world is confined to their small apartment, mainly the kitchen, where she rustles up delectable dishes). Saajan is a widower on the verge of retirement. They are both desperately lonely. The lunchbox that travels between them, ensconced in a dull green tiffin cover, becomes a lifeline for them both. Through it, they probe and prod and imperceptibly alter each other. Something shifts in Ila and Saajan. They decide to demand more of life.

Ritesh, who also wrote the screenplay, tells this story with unforced tenderness. In a city of more than 20 million, fate brings these two people together. The film suggests they are connected by something elemental. So in one scene, Saajan shoos away a fly and it cuts to Ila doing the same. Hindi film music binds them. Saajan commutes on the local train, in which children begging for alms are singing 'Pardesi Pardesi' from *Raja Hindustani*. The shot cuts to the same song playing on the radio in Ila's house. Later in the film, she is listening to '*Mera Dil Bhi*' from *Saajan*, which then seamlessly transitions to the children on the train singing the same song.

Much of Saajan's life is spent standing, uncomfortably close to strangers, on buses and trains that take him back and forth to a job he has held for thirty-five years—without, as his boss tells us, making a single mistake. At one point, he writes to Ila: 'When my wife died, she got a horizontal burial plot. I tried to buy a burial plot for myself the other day, and what they offered me was a vertical one. I spend my whole life standing in trains and buses, and now I'll have to stand even when I'm dead.' In a quiet, unhurried manner, the film captures the oppressive frenzy

of Mumbai. *The Lunchbox* is a portrait of loneliness, peppered
with elegant silences and moments of breath-taking loveliness.
In another letter, Saajan writes: 'I think we forget things if we
have no one to tell them to.'

Saajan has a hard and brittle exterior (the office gossip is
that he once kicked a cat who was then run over by a bus).
Which is perhaps why, in the crowded canteen, he always has
his lunch alone. Ila penetrates his armour with her delicious
food and her notes, which are clear-eyed and searching. Aslam
Shaikh, his junior, penetrates it with relentless good cheer.
Played with endearing enthusiasm by Nawazuddin Siddiqui,
Aslam is the perfect foil to Saajan. He's hopeful, sociable
and determined to squeeze every ounce of happiness out of
his straitened circumstances. The scenes between Aslam and
Saajan have a tinge of sweetness that will make you smile. It's a
joy to watch two actors of this calibre play off each other.

But even the more joyful scenes in the film are suffused
with sadness. The protagonists are bruised people battling their
solitude, which is constantly being underlined by the crowded
city. Irrfan's riveting performance encapsulates this sadness.
His eyes are wise and weary. Even when Saajan smiles, you
can sense fatigue. Ila, though younger, carries that same burden
of joylessness. Nimrat Kaur imbues her with the right balance
of dignity and desperation. When Ila writes to Saajan about
a woman who committed suicide with her child, you know
instantly that Ila is capable of doing the same.

Food is also a character in *The Lunchbox*. It connects people.
Ila's faceless neighbour Mrs Deshpande (whom we hear but never
see), exchanges recipes and spices with her. Aslam feeds Saajan
his signature lamb dish. Aslam is Muslim, Saajan is Catholic and
Ila is Hindu. But this is never underlined or commented on. The
three are bound together by a shared humanity.

The Lunchbox doesn't tell us what happens to Ila and Saajan. In 2016, I did an interview with Ritesh in which I asked how he imagined their lives turned out. He said he didn't know. But I do. In my version, Ila and Saajan move to Bhutan—a country that fascinates Ila because of its focus on gross national happiness rather than gross national product.

Bhutan is one of my favourite places on the planet and the fact that it is Ila's fantasy escape made me like *The Lunchbox* even more. It is a country of such startling beauty that I can't imagine anyone could be unhappy there. So I think of Ila and Saajan and Ila's daughter together, watching the sun set behind the high mountains and savouring Ila's cooking—especially brinjal, which Saajan insists on calling aubergine.

Ritesh Batra is too sophisticated a storyteller to spin a 'happily ever after'. But I think Ila and Saajan find a semblance of serenity.

You can watch *The Lunchbox* on Netflix.

4

Tungrus

I don't drink but I think of short films like tequila shots: bracing, heady, quick. There is little room for plots or emotions to brew. The pleasure is immediate.

In March 2014, the *New Yorker*'s film critic Richard Brody wrote, in an article titled 'Does the Cinema Need Short Films?', that the 'most significant critical work on the subject of the short film' is Jean-Luc Godard's report in the French film magazine *Cahiers du Cinema*. Brody said that Godard, writing about the short film festival in Tours in 1958, called the format the 'anti-cinema'. He argued that 'a short film does not have time to think. It therefore belongs to that impure cinema to which André Bazin wished a long life: with good reason, moreover, since through this very impurity it enables, *a contrario*, many directors to prove their talent. So the short film is useful to the cinema in a way, but like the antibody in medicine'.

One of my favourite short films is *Tungrus and the Chicken From Hell*. The duration of the film is only 12 minutes and

36 seconds, but in this brief time, debutant director Rishi Chandna creates comedy, family drama, and even a touch of tragedy. *Tungrus* . . . is about a middle-class family in Mumbai. One day, the father comes home with a chick. They don't expect that it will live long, but six months later, it is a full-grown rooster who terrorizes their two cats and other family members. As the father, Nusrat Bharde, puts it: '*Yeh toh* don *ban gaya.*'

There's something inherently comedic about a rooster clucking and excreting all over a cramped Mumbai apartment. The bird eats everything, including chicken. He crows incessantly. The only way to stop him is to chase him, which Nusrat does with enthusiasm. Nusrat's wife says he reminds her of the character Tungrus (played by Naseeruddin Shah) in Shyam Benegal's 1983 film *Mandi*. Which is where the film gets its name. Nusrat is the most sanguine member of the family. He grew up in a village, around animals, and is comfortable with the idea that they eventually will eat the rooster. His grown sons dislike their pet (one says, 'I don't see what a rooster can add to a household'), but they can't get used to the idea of cooking and eating him.

Rishi builds the belligerent rooster into a fascinating character, but tones down the inherent drama of the story, telling it straight and without embellishment. There is no handheld camera chasing the rooster. Instead we get classical visual language in which the camera stays still but the rooster is constantly moving. The cinematography by Deepak Nambiar and editing by Neha Mehra are first-rate. Each moment is precise and makes a pertinent point about this frankly absurd situation. The humour is leavened by a layer of sadness. In one scene, Mr and Mrs Bharde are petting the rooster as though he were a dog. They've raised him but now can't agree on what should come next.

Tungrus . . . played at dozens of film festivals and won several awards, including the Grand Jury Prize for Best Short

Documentary at the Slamdance Film Festival in Utah in 2019 and the Audience Award in international competition at the Glasgow Short Film Festival in the same year. The film was eventually picked up by the *New York Times* and resides in its Op-Docs section. The chicken from hell found a global audience—a fitting tribute to a memorable bird.

5

Angamaly Diaries

Angamaly is a small town located north of Kochi in Kerala. The Malayalam film *Angamaly Diaries* (2017) is about the lives of the people who live there. Which sounds prosaic and perhaps even un-cinematic. But from this material, director Lijo Jose Pellissery fashions a furious rollercoaster of a film. He doesn't just take us to Angamaly. He soaks us in its sights, sounds and smells: there are so many close-ups of food that you can almost inhale the aromas. Movies are often described as an inexpensive way to travel the world. Few Indian films have transported me to a new place as completely as this one did.

The sensory overload begins with the opening credits. A series of quick cuts introduces us to a church, busy streets, railway crossing, telephone exchange, religious processions, cop directing traffic, meats being fried and cooked in vast vats, small hotels and cinemas, nuns walking on a busy road, and more. It's a frenzied introduction. Even if you've never heard of the place (I hadn't), you become a local instantly.

Angamaly Diaries is designed to look scrappy and un-designed. As Lijo said in an interview, you don't feel like you're watching cinema. The cast consists of eighty-six newcomers, all of whom feel like they belong on these streets. The film is narrated by Vincent Pepe (played by the charming Antony Varghese), who breaks the fourth wall and looks at us as his voiceover starts with: 'I am an Angamalian.' Vincent narrates his story, beginning from when he was a choirboy at the local church. He grows up idolizing one of the local goons and, taking a cue from him, forms his own gang, which is called the Palliyangadi Team. These aren't hardcore criminals, even though they occasionally throw bombs and carry guns. The bombs they use are homemade—the guy making them embraces a tree while doing it, so that if something goes wrong and the bomb explodes in his hands, the damage will be contained.

The film is peppered with such black comedy. In another scene, we are at a funeral being attended by both the wife and the mistress of the deceased and the mistress is wailing much more than the wife. It turns out that his body won't fit in the coffin, so a few quick karate chops are administered to break bones and squeeze it in.

Even the violence has strains of comedy—early on in the film, a fight breaks out in a bar and involves men dressed up as Jesus, a Roman soldier and a nun. One minute, the men are knocking back drinks. The next, they are punching and kicking. If feels like a scene from the Gaul village of the Asterix comics.

There's plenty of carnage in *Angamaly Diaries*. Vincent and his team face off against a tougher gang led by the brothers Ravi and Rajan, who have served time in jail for murder and now rule Angamaly's thriving pork trade. Ravi and Rajan teach Vincent and his gang how to make money hand over fist with pigs, but the two teams fall out when Vincent's people start undercutting their mentors. Their battle spills out onto the streets and eventually leads to death and murder in Angamaly.

The story might be grim but the telling never becomes sombre. The narrative continues in its scrappy, charming way, taking time to educate us on the delicacies of the town—we are told that the best 'parotta and beef fry in Angamaly is at the Paris Hotel, best omelette is at Kunju's street-food joint and best biryani is at Thachil hotel'. The enmity between the gangs isn't set in stone either—once they sort out their differences, they start making plans to have drinks together. The brawling and the posturing don't stem from any deep-seated ideological differences. They're just a way of life.

This is, of course, an extremely male world. Women—wives, sisters, girlfriends—make only fleeting appearances. They stand on the sidelines while the men create mayhem. All of which culminates in a bravura, climactic, 11-minute, single-shot sequence that fuses religion and violence. Lijo and cinematographer Girish Gangadharan create a dazzling set-piece—the camera snakes in and out of homes and through a religious procession; the men fight and stab, firecrackers go off and ultimately, people die. The exhilarating action of *Angamaly Diaries* is accompanied by composer Prashant Pillai's propulsive score. It underlines the highly combustible nature of these people.

There is something primal about these men—in the scenes in which pigs are being slaughtered, you sense their almost guttural need for violence. Lijo went on to explore this in greater detail in a later film, *Jallikattu* (2019). Here, he doesn't let the mood get too dark. After all, it's Angamaly and there's always some fun to be had.

You can watch the film on Netflix.

6

Chak De! India

Some films we watch for the tale. Others we watch for the telling. Sports films generally fall in the latter category. These movies work like comfort food. Their beat is familiar and the lack of surprises is one of their pleasures. We know the end before we begin—the underdog will vanquish insurmountable odds and win—but that doesn't make the victory any less sweet. Sports films celebrate the triumph of the will, and in Bollywood, few films have done this with the aplomb of *Chak De! India*.

Director Shimit Amin and writer Jaideep Sahni construct a straightforward narrative: even before the opening credits are over, Kabir Khan, captain of the men's hockey team and Asia's best centre forward, has gone from being an admired sportsman to a disgraced has-been whose effigies are being burnt in the streets. It is believed that he threw a game against Pakistan, allowing them to win the World Cup, because his allegiances lie there. In the first few minutes, the stakes are established—we know that Kabir is innocent and that he is on trial because he is Muslim. A Rahul or a Raj would have suffered the ignominy of defeat but would never have been accused of being a traitor. We understand that Kabir will have to work a miracle to clear his name and prove his loyalty to his country.

Chak De! India (2007) was the first time Shah Rukh Khan played a Muslim on screen, barring a brief cameo in Kamal Haasan's *Hey Ram*. Kabir's religion is the pivot of the story but Shimit doesn't hammer the point home. We never see Kabir doing the namaz. He never says he is Muslim. Throughout the film, he wears Western clothes. Shimit layers his identity into the narrative—in the *aadab* that Kabir greets people with; in the Urdu prayer you see on the exteriors of his home as he leaves it with his mother, neighbours standing and staring, unwilling to help; in the way Kabir says '*Khuda*' during the climactic speech; or in the Sufi song '*Maula Mere Le Le Meri Jaan*', composed by Salim Merchant and Sulaiman Merchant, which plays in the background at key moments. Kabir is fully cognisant of what has caused his downfall but he never spells it out. So when his former teammate says, '*Ek galti toh sabko maaf hoti hai*,' Kabir only asks ruefully, '*Sabko?*'

Once Kabir's tragic situation is set up, the odds against him are rolled out. We meet the ragtag women's hockey team that Kabir has sworn to lead to the World Cup. One character calls them the '*rakshason ki sena*'. Another dismisses the team as 'a formality', saying they aren't even good enough to play against high-school teams from Europe.

Kabir's friend tells him frankly: '*Yeh* team *nahi, kabr hai.*' There's an assortment of states, languages, personality types. Among them, Balbir (played by Tanya Abrol), the hot-headed, bulldog Punjaban who never backs away from a fight; Komal (Chitrashi Rawat), the no-nonsense Haryanvi who is still learning how to be a team player; Bindia (Shilpa Shukla), the defiant senior player who memorably inspires Kabir to deliver that killer line: '*Har* team *mein sirf ek hi gunda ho sakta hai aur iss* team *ka gunda main hoon*'; Preeti (Sagarika Ghatge), who is dating an entitled cricket player, but dumps him with such aplomb during the end credits that you want to cheer; and the women from Jharkhand—Rani Dispotta (Seema Azmi) and Soimoi Kerketa (Nisha Nair)—with their determination and their distinctive tales.

Through the course of the film, these women learn to be world-class players. But when Kabir first meets them, their talent is undermined by their rawness, their prickly personalities and their unwillingness to be part of a larger vision. Each one is aligned to her state. In one of the film's best scenes, Kabir impresses upon them that they are no longer playing for Haryana or Punjab or Karnataka. They are playing for India. So when each woman steps forward to introduce herself, it must no longer be with the name of her state, but with the name of her country. They begin to understand what he means when he says: '*Mujhe* states *ke naam na sunaai dete hain, na dikhai dete hain. Sirf ek mulk ka naam sunaai deta hai:* India.'

Chak De! India wears its patriotism on its sleeve. When the film's name first appears in the opening credits, green and orange strategically streak through the white lettering. Once Kabir accepts the seemingly doomed assignment of coaching this team, he drives off on his scooter against a silhouette of India Gate. His personal quest is suffused with a larger nationalism. This isn't merely about hockey or winning. This is about upholding an idea of India. Later in the film, just before the women's World Cup final against Australia, Kabir is alone in the stadium, watching the Indian tricolour being raised for the game. The captain of the team, Vidya Sharma (Vidya Malvade), asks him what he's doing. He replies, '*Pehli baar kisi gore ko India ka tiranga lehrate hue dekh raha hoon.*'

Visually, *Chak De! India* has little varnish, which was a departure for its production house, Yash Raj Films. Until then, the studio was known largely for glossy romances featuring A-list stars. This time, aside from Shah Rukh, the film had no known faces, no glamour. Shimit gives us a few aerial shots of the landscape when we first get to Australia, but he doesn't exploit the foreign location in the way YRF films usually do. The textures are naturalistic but the director combines this with the dramatic beats of a Bollywood film. The dialogue and screenplay (also by Jaideep) are designed to land punches and rouse the audience.

Post interval, the women's team is pitted against the men's—they have to prove their competence in order to earn the trip to Australia for the World Cup. The women lose, but their spirit and talent are acknowledged as the men raise their hockey sticks in respect. It's a moment that makes you tear up, and we aren't even near the crescendo.

The film determinedly celebrates women. Most of the male characters are condescending and casually dismissive of both the team's game and their dream of winning the World Cup. Preeti's fiancé isn't the only one who thinks it's a joke. Early on in the film, a Hockey Federation member sniggers and says, '*Yeh chakla belan chalane wali kya* hockey stick *chalayengi.*'

The women's game has no sponsors or spectators. Kabir is their lone champion. Off-screen, so are Shimit and Jaideep. Midway through the film, they construct a fabulous, free-for-all brawl in which the women get together and beat up men who were making lewd remarks at some of their teammates. Every woman alive has had the latter experience; few have had the former. So to watch these women unite in rage at these offenders is as satisfying as any of their victories on the field.

You could argue that the film's feminist stance is specious because ultimately Kabir is the male saviour, constantly pushing and inspiring the women to fight the odds, their circumstances and their worst instincts (at one point, Bindia offers to sleep with him if he will make her captain). Perhaps. But Shah Rukh plays the role so persuasively that I'm willing to make peace with that.

I think *Chak De! India* is one of his finest performances. We get India's biggest romantic star shorn of romance, vanity, glamour, even his signature stylized mannerisms—there is no opportunity for the outstretched arms because the love story is between Kabir and hockey, Kabir and his country, Kabir and his quest for victory.

Shah Rukh, handsome but frayed, finds the hollowness and ache in Kabir. His eyes reflect the humiliation of his own defeat, the scars he carries like a shield. So when the women win the World Cup, Kabir doesn't jump or cheer. Instead, he staggers back, almost like he's been struck. Before this win, Kabir delivers the memorable '*Sattar* minute' monologue. The sports film's climactic locker-room speech might be a cliché, but this is one of the best examples. It's not long and yet it delivers. Kabir urges the women 'to play the best hockey of their lives'. He tells them that if they do that, it won't matter if they win or lose; no one can take those 70 minutes away from them. He inspires them to be their best selves.

I wish we could all have a coach like Kabir. You can watch *Chak De! India* on Amazon Prime and on YouTube.

7

Chashme Buddoor

Miss Chamko. For people of a certain vintage, that name will instantly elicit a smile and memories of Deepti Naval as Neha, selling laundry detergent. *'Baar baar, lagaataar, Chamko!'* she says, in such delightful earnest that the gleaming bubbles she has rustled up in her bucket pale in comparison.

Neha is giving a demonstration to a young Delhi University student named Siddharth (played by a disarmingly handsome Farooq Shaikh). Could a man and a woman meet under more ordinary circumstances? And yet, the writing and the actors have a sweetness that hasn't faded over the decades. The coy glances, awkwardness and humour—when she pulls out the towel after a five-minute soak and remarks how clean it is, and he says, of course, I gave you a clean one—make this a classic meet-cute.

The same situation in a contemporary film might be unsettling: a woman alone with a stranger in his apartment. In fact, quite a few narrative threads in *Chashme Buddoor* now seem problematic: Siddharth's roommates, Omi and Jomo, played by Rakesh Bedi and Ravi Baswani, chase any woman they see, designating them all '*shikaar*'. They are stalkers and liars who falsely malign a woman because they made no headway in their pursuit of her. A grandmother happily participates in the charade of having her granddaughter kidnapped so that she can be rescued by her boyfriend and then reunited with him. It's logic-free. And yet, *Chashme Buddoor* chips away at your resistance because the film is suffused with charm and innocence.

Writer-director Sai Paranjpye immerses us in a kinder world, one reminiscent of the gentle comedies of Hrishikesh Mukherjee (who, incidentally, is the signatory on the censor certificate—he was then chairman of the board). '*Chashm-e-buddoor*' translates loosely from its Persian origins as 'May you be far from evil', and that's precisely the texture of this film. These are ordinary people enjoying moments of friendship, laughter, music, love. Saeed Jaffrey, terrific as the local cigarette-shop owner Lalan Mian, is sometimes stern with these three roommates who are constantly buying on *udhaar*. But his aggression goes only so far as threatening to take a favourite new record away from Omi and Jomo. There are no dark undertones here. Even the villain is comically ineffectual.

Early in the film, Lalan Mian says, '*Yahaan toh saara kaam nek iraadon pe hi chal raha hai.*' And that's perhaps why *Chashme Buddoor* endures—because we can sense that it comes from a place of good intent. The film was released in 1981, the same year as mainstream Hindi hits such as *Laawaris*, *Love Story* and *Ek Hi Bhool*. There was little conversation then around the portrayal of women, or indeed men, love and the chase, as depicted in Hindi cinema; heroines were largely ornamental. In that environment, Sai created a film that worked as a frothy take on love and friendship, and as a clever critique of this kind of Hindi cinema.

Her screenplay uses the tropes of mainstream movies and pokes fun at them. Omi and Jomo both try to befriend Neha and fail, so they make up stories about what happened when they went to her house. Omi sees himself as a poet singing a duet—the lilting '*Is Nadi Ko Mera*', composed by Raj Kamal— with Neha on a boat. It's a typical Hindi film romantic situation. Jomo's narrative is like a mini-film, in which he gets beaten up by goons who are trying to kidnap Neha. These sequences are constructed as artifice. In the climactic action sequence, Omi even says, 'Villain saab, *bhagwan ke liye humein chhod do.*' Sai is laughing, with affection, at the dominant narratives of the day.

Her screenplay also underlines the contrast between how things happen in the movies and how they happen in real life. At some point in the film, Amitabh Bachchan and Rekha make an appearance as themselves. Mr Bachchan flirts with and of course gets Rekha. When Jomo tries this method of pretending to return a handkerchief that a woman has dropped, his intended *shikaar* simply takes it and keeps walking. It's hilarious.

It's telling that Omi and Jomo never get the women they pursue. They get used by women who are clearly smarter than they are (one girl accepts the offer of a ride with Jomo, directs him to where she wants to go, then hops off and runs to her boyfriend). In fact, the only one who succeeds in finding love is Siddharth, the idealist who has photos of Gandhiji on his wall and who barely speaks to women because he is so immersed in study (he is inordinately proud of his 'MA with distinction').

Farooq Shaikh, radiating decency, is pitch-perfect as Siddharth. His clumsiness in wooing Neha is particularly attractive—during her detergent demonstration, he casually suggests they let it soak five minutes extra and then insists that she eat some *laddu*, which he offers to her in a coffee mug. This is the kind of man every woman can feel safe with, which is perhaps why within five minutes of meeting him, she gives him the details of her music classes so he can meet her again.

Chashme Buddoor will make you nostalgic for a time of fewer complications and certainly far less traffic. One of the joys of watching the film is seeing the empty streets of New Delhi and the lush trees. Siddharth and Neha's first date is at a restaurant nestled amid greenery. When Siddharth asks the waiter what's good, he replies '*Mahaul*', the atmosphere. That's true of this film too. You might suddenly find yourself longing for the tutti-frutti ice cream that Neha has every time they meet. I wonder if anyone makes it anymore.

You can watch *Chashme Buddoor* on Amazon Prime and on YouTube.

8

Dil Chahta Hai

I believe that cool officially arrived in Bollywood with *Dil Chahta Hai*. When the rhythms of the title song kicked in, with the shots of the road running underneath, the trees swaying overhead and the three young men—Akash, Sameer and Sid—driving to Goa in that Mercedes convertible, something fundamental shifted. Even if you didn't have their youthful insouciance or their affluence, you aspired to have their bonding, their freedom, aspired to that feeling the song evoked of timeless friendship. It was a different sort of magic.

Farhan Akhtar's debut film broke every rule in the book. As another song in the film put it, '*Hum hain naye, andaaz kyun ho purana.*' It was a coming-of-age story with characters who felt refreshingly like people we could know—these young men, Tara Jaiswal (played by a glorious Dimple Kapadia), Mahesh Uncle in Australia (Rajat Kapoor), the agonizingly boring but unforgettable Subodh (who was a slave to his timetable), were all regular people. They weren't larger-than-life or impossibly

29

rich and attractive. For the first time, young, modern, urban Indians saw a version of themselves on screen. The relationships between the three friends—the banter, the joking and laughter, the comfortable silences—seemed plucked from life. Akash, Sameer and Sid didn't proclaim their friendship in the manner of earlier Hindi-film heroes (think Veeru and Jai in *Sholay*). There was no need. Their relationship was understood.

As was the relationship between Sid and Tara, the most sensitively crafted thread in the film. Sid is an artist—literally (he's a painter), but also by temperament. Tara is older and more frayed. She's been bruised badly by the cards life has dealt her. But Farhan, who was only twenty-seven when the film released in 2001, doesn't allow us to pity her. Tara is an independent working woman with strength and elegance. She is an alcoholic who never loses her dignity. We can see why Sid falls in love with her. But he demands nothing in return. He doesn't even tell her. At the end, Tara says to Sid, '*Kuch rishtey hote hain jinka koi naam nahi hota.*' Which took me back to one of Gulzar's finest songs, '*Hamne Dekhi Hai Un Ankhon Ki*', from the 1969 film *Khamoshi*. He wrote, '*Sirf ehsaas hai yeh rooh se mehsoos karo, pyar ko pyar hi rehne do koi naam na do.*'

Dil Chahta Hai is about the transformative power of love. The three friends grow up through the course of the film. Akash undergoes the biggest evolution. When we first meet him, he's cocky and callous. He's also very funny. But even as you laugh at his antics, you recognize that brittle edge that can cut when he goes too far—as he does with Sid.

Sameer is the easy-going one, keeping peace between the two. Akash only understands Sid's emotions and the hurt he's caused when he falls in love with Shalini (Preity Zinta)—this is perhaps the only Hindi film in which a leading man realizes the depth of his emotions while at the opera (*Troilus and Cressida*, no less). The man who treats the very idea of love with disdain is later forced to bare his emotions in front of 300 people. Aamir Khan makes this change of heart entirely convincing. Through the film, you can see his abrasive nature softening. When Akash sits alone in his Sydney apartment, weeping from loneliness, the ache is palpable. Akshaye Khanna as Sid dials it down—his performance is contained in expressions, gestures, half-smiles and silences. There is no theatricality. Saif Ali Khan as the dazed and confused Sameer is the perfect foil for these two. His goofball charm carries him through.

Akash's declaration of love at Shalini's *sangeet* is one of the few times, I felt, that *Dil Chahta Hai* faltered. After creating a new tonality for Bollywood storytelling, Farhan went *filmi* on us. The sequence is emotionally unconvincing. But he finds his grip again with Sameer cracking a joke about this proposal— because among friends, everything is fodder for comedy.

Dil Chahta Hai is laugh-out-loud funny. And when these three laugh at each other, you become one of the gang because the camaraderie is so lived-in, and these situations, so relatable. *Dil Chahta Hai* might be slice-of-life, but it's not ordinary. The production design by Suzanne Caplan Merwanji, the trend-setting hairdos by Avan Contractor and the styling by Arjun Bhasin gave the film an urbane, fashion-forward sheen that was aspirational without being intimidating. Designer labels weren't on display here as they were, for instance, in *Kuch Kuch Hota Hai*, but every element in the frame was part of a distinctive aesthetic—down to the lined wallpaper in Tara's home.

The film's enduring success is also powered by the song sequences: tunes by Shankar-Ehsaan-Loy, lyrics by Javed Akhtar and choreography by Farah Khan. '*Woh Ladki Hai Kahan*', in which Sameer and Pooja go to a movie and see themselves enacting songs in Hindi film set-ups through the decades, is a thing of beauty. As is '*Koi Kahe Kehta Rahe*'.

In an interview in 2017, Farhan told me that he has a distinct memory from the shoot for that song. It was filmed at Famous Studio and one evening, as he was returning home, accompanied by some of his crew and Preity Zinta, she turned to him and said emphatically, 'You know, Farhan, this is going to be a cult movie.' He said she was the only one who thought that before the film came out. Others had less faith. It's hard to imagine now, but some distributors saw the finished movie and rescinded their deals because they didn't think it would run.

My most distinct memory of *Dil Chahta Hai* is from the preview that Farhan and his business partner Ritesh Sidhwani held at the same Famous Studio. My husband Vidhu Vinod Chopra and I talked about the film all the way home. We both loved it. Neither of us knew Farhan very well, but Vinod wanted to call Farhan's mother Honey Irani and congratulate her. It was past 1 a.m., but I encouraged him to do it. I said that if someone were calling to gush about my son's first film, I would want them to wake me up. And that's exactly what Vinod did. She was very pleased to hear from him.

Preity was right. *Dil Chahta Hai* became a cult classic and the anthem of a generation. You can watch the film on Amazon Prime.

9

Don

'Don *ka intezaar toh gyarah mulkon ki* police *kar rahi hai lekin ek baat samajh lo,* Don *ko pakadna mushkil hi nahi, namumkin hai.*' You probably associate this line with Shah Rukh Khan, in shades and leather jacket, chewing up the scenery as a dreaded international criminal. But for viewers of a certain generation, there is only one Don: Amitabh Bachchan.

Twenty-eight years before Farhan Akhtar's remake, Mr Bachchan, director Chandra Barot and writers Salim-Javed were redefining cool without the aid of foreign locations, snazzy special effects or gadgetry. The original *Don* is a testament to talent, with terrific writing, a crackling soundtrack (by Kalyanji-Anandji) and a performer at the top of his game. Mr Bachchan, in a double role, is in almost every frame. And he's equally persuasive as both the suave smuggler Don and the '*Ganga-kinare wala chhora*' Vijay who impersonates him.

Mr Bachchan plays the former with practised panache and the latter with cheerful enthusiasm. He makes them both charismatic and delectably watchable. Many elements of the film haven't dated well (like Pran's wig and monogrammed shirts—his character is named Jasjit so he has JJ embroidered on his pockets), but Mr Bachchan's double role is a thing of beauty.

As Don, he cultivates an air of being resolutely unfazed—nothing shakes that implacable king-of-the-world expression. In *The Silence of the Lambs*, we are told that Hannibal Lecter's pulse doesn't go over eighty-five even when he attacks a nurse and eats her tongue. Don is far too slick for such grotesque gestures, but I suspect that his pulse doesn't flutter much either.

In the first scene, we see Don driving a swanky red car to a business meeting in the middle of an open field. He's wearing a three-piece suit, a giant red bowtie and rather daring yellow glares. When his customers try to double-cross him, he kills them, quite casually, by tossing a briefcase filled with explosives at them. Later, in his den, he shoots a man who works for him, then pours himself a whiskey and says to the other gaping gang members, 'Cheers, gentlemen.' Of course, the man Don murdered turns out to be a police informer with a list of contacts hidden in the heel of his shoe. Don doesn't make mistakes.

My favourite moment in this smooth criminal act is Don's interaction with Kamini (played by a scintillating Helen). Kamini attempts to seduce Don so she can have him captured by the police, because Don murdered her lover. We see them in a post-coital conversation—he, still lying in bed, asks her, '*Kya naam bataya tumne apna?*' and later proceeds to declare, 'Romantic *baatein mujhe bahut* bore *karti hain.*' When the police arrive, Don doesn't panic. He simply uses Kamini to escape by taking her hostage and then kills her. His malevolence and his wardrobe (this is a criminal who wears suits and ties to work) both reek of sophistication.

In sharp contrast, his doppelganger, the good-hearted Vijay, is a naïve bumpkin whose greatest joy is chewing *paan*.

He's in awe of '*Bambai nagariya*'. Circumstances force him to take the place of Don (whom he refers to as 'Daaaan'). Vijay impersonating Don, then breaking character and becoming Vijay, is one of the highlights of the film. Mr Bachchan revels in the double act. Consider the classic song '*Khaike Paan Banaraswala*'. Mr Bachchan posted on Twitter that it was in fact 'An after thought, that became THE thought'. The song was shot after the film had been completed. Media reports say it was added because filmmaker Manoj Kumar, who saw rushes of *Don*, declared that the film was so gripping that audiences wouldn't be able to take a toilet break. Hence a song to relieve the non-stop tension.

I'm not sure that worked, because '*Khaike Paan Banaraswala*' is irresistible. It's hard to imagine that anyone would choose to leave their seat while it was playing. The song is an item number—it doesn't further the narrative in any way—but it has context. After days of being Don, Vijay gets to be himself amid a group of *paan*-chewing, *bhang*-swilling *dhobis*. He tells them, '*Tohre mulk ke hain*,' downs a few glasses and then breaks into song. Mr Bachchan's hip-swivelling dance is infused with an infectious energy. It doesn't even seem choreographed. He swivels with such abandon that it feels like nothing matters except this brief moment of unadulterated happiness. Even the '*memsahib*' Roma joins in.

Roma is a unique leading lady. In the late 1970s, women were largely slotted as either romantic partners, sacrificing mothers, or sisters who got raped (giving heroes a motive for revenge). The woman's main function was to add visual allure, which Zeenat Aman certainly does. But with *Haré Rama Haré Krishna* in 1971, Zeenat had upended the notion of the Hindi film heroine. Her imposing height and svelte physique brought in a Western sensibility and redefined notions of glamour.

As Roma, she's no simpering beauty queen either. She's a fighter who goes after Don when her brother is killed. She participates equally in the action. In the climactic free-for-all in which Vijay, Roma and Jasjit go up against the bad guys, Roma literally kicks ass. She beats up as many baddies as the men do. It's exhilarating to watch. But even here, Chandra Barot keeps the humour intact. Vijay stops the fighting to put a *paan* in his mouth and then, with red lips, continues to beat his opponents.

The film never takes itself too seriously. *Don* is the ultimate entertainer and it doesn't let up.

Expectedly, it was one of the biggest hits of 1978. The fast-paced plot and numerous thrills were lapped up by audiences. The film doesn't deliver the same way today, of course, but *Don* has moments of euphoria that still connect. More than anything, *Don* provides a front-row seat to the dazzling talent of Amitabh Bachchan.

You can watch the film on YouTube.

10

Duniya Na Mane

I first heard about *Duniya Na Mane* from my mother, Kamna Chandra. She told me that she had seen the film when she was a little girl, but it made such an impact on her that she still remembered the goosebumps she had while watching it. I thought she was being dramatic (after all, she is a scriptwriter). But then I watched the film myself.

Duniya Na Mane was made by V. Shantaram in 1937. Film historian B.D. Garga described it as 'Indian cinema's first uncompromising social statement, which, without becoming a dull reform tract, was also exciting cinema'. Essentially, this film is the ancestor of all the message movies we see—especially those focused on women's empowerment. At the time of its release, *Duniya Na Mane* was nothing short of revolutionary. And all these decades later, Shantaram's ferocious push against patriarchy still resonates.

Duniya Na Mane, which was shot and released simultaneously in Marathi as *Kunku*, is based on the novel *Na Patnari Goshta* by Narayan Hari Apte, who also wrote the script. The film is about an orphaned young girl, Nirmala, who is tricked and sold by her avaricious uncle into marriage with a much older man. The difference in their ages is so great that Nirmala's husband Keshavlal has children the same age as his new wife.

But Nirmala refuses to play the victim. Her dissent begins at the wedding: she refuses to pose for the wedding photograph. In her husband's home, she is purposefully defiant and rude. When the elderly *chachi* who lives with them asks her to take a cup of tea to Keshavlal, she refuses. When the neighbouring women come to see her, she says, '*Main badi buri ladki hoon.*' She refuses to share a bedroom with her husband and declares, '*Zaroor dukh sahungi magar anyaya nahi bardasht karungi.*' She fights back verbally and even physically, saying that her aim is to make her husband's family so miserable that it will make other families think twice before ruining another girl's life.

Nirmala is a groundbreaking character and Shanta Apte plays her with a steely dignity. She is vulnerable and tragic, but also heroic in her refusal to make peace with her awful circumstances. The brilliance of the film is that it doesn't demonize Keshavlal either. He starts out as a vain patriarch who thinks nothing of buying himself a new bride. He dyes his moustache and believes that he is young again. But Nirmala's resolve and strength force him to reconsider his behaviour. Shantaram depicts this evolution brilliantly—an old clock hanging in Keshavlal's room becomes a metaphor. It keeps stopping, which starts to haunt him because he fears the same thing will happen with his heart. There is almost no background music, but Shantaram uses sound and shadows to depict the state of mind of this lonely old man. At the end, he is so ashamed of his actions that he wipes Nirmala's *sindoor* away himself and says, '*Tera pati hone ke kaabil main nahi hoon.*'

These ideas were pathbreaking but *Duniya Na Mane* also offers complex characters and sophisticated writing. You will have to adjust to the inherent theatricality of the storytelling, and the frequent songs—this includes an English one named *A Psalm of Life*, sung by Apte herself. But there is courage and artistry here that are inspiring.

You can watch the film on YouTube.

11

Hazaaron Khwaishein Aisi

Poetry and politics is a blend rarely found in Hindi cinema, but Sudhir Mishra's 2005 film *Hazaaron Khwaishein Aisi* is an exception.

It is a romance that plays out at many levels. The plot pivots around the fraught love triangle involving the three principal characters: Siddharth, Geeta and Vikram. But the film is also about the romance of idealism, of revolution, of an idea of India. The story begins in 1969 and ends in 1975, against the backdrop of the Emergency. The social turbulence is mirrored by emotional turbulence. There is violence and corruption, desire and infidelity, greed and oppression. And ultimately, ideologies— Leftist, Marxist, capitalist and opportunist—prove too narrow to encapsulate the messiness and unpredictability of life.

The *khwaishein* of the title, taken from one of Mirza Ghalib's most famous poems, remain unfulfilled.

We first meet Siddharth, Geeta and Vikram just as they are finishing college in Delhi. Siddharth, from an affluent and accomplished family (his father is a judge), dreams of toppling the corrupt establishment by any means necessary. In a letter to Geeta, he says he wants to 'end the vulgarity of oppression', adding, 'The violence of the oppressed is right. The violence of the oppressor is wrong. And to hell with ethics.'

Geeta, who has lived between the UK and New Delhi, loves Siddharth but doesn't share his passion for fixing the fractured country. She's never been to a village and can't summon up the enthusiasm that Siddharth has for rebellion. Vikram, who loves Geeta, doesn't understand Siddharth either. Vikram's father is a Gandhian but all Vikram wants is to get rich quick. He writes to Geeta that he can't understand 'rich kids playing the let's-change-the-world game'. He says, 'While you are looking for a way out, I am looking for a way in.'

In *Hazaaron Khwaishein Aisi*, Sudhir and his co-writers, Shivkumar Subramaniam, Ruchi Narain and Sanjay Chauhan, construct a film that is cognisant of the atrocities of the state and sympathetic to the Naxal cause. The system, which is served and exploited by fixers like Vikram, is rotten. But the narrative also reveals the naïveté and inherent contradictions of some of the rebels.

Early in the film, we get a party scene in which Siddharth's college mate gestures at the sprawling bungalow behind them and declares: 'I'm sorry, I still believe in the ideology but my dad is too rich. I can't give up all this, can I?' The humour is bitter and biting. In another scene, a rich landlord in the village who is having a heart attack agrees to be treated by a lower-caste doctor but his son objects furiously. It's potent, dark and absurdly funny.

Revolution requires blood, sweat and patience. In rural Bihar, which Siddharth says is separated from Delhi 'by 5,000 years', the more things change, the more they stay the same. The horrors of caste, the police brutality and the utter lawlessness make it difficult to implement change. Siddharth, Geeta and Vikram confront the heart of darkness and come away permanently scarred. At the end, as the mournful *'Baawra Mann'* (sung beautifully by lyricist Swanand Kirkire) plays in the background, there is a semblance of peace, but a just world seems as far away as it was when the story began.

Hazaaron Khwaishein Aisi breaks many showbiz rules. It's a Hindi film in which the characters speak mostly English—not the archly accented or theatrical kind either, but the natural sound of urban India. It's a low-budget film made without any stars. (Chitrangda Singh and Shiney Ahuja were both found via screen tests. Kay Kay Menon was the only recognizable face.) It was composer Shantanu Moitra and Swanand's first film. Swanand also served as assistant to the director.

There were media reports that several actresses rejected the role of Geeta because the character was sexually liberated (even after marriage, Geeta continues her affair with Siddharth). Which is just as well. Because Chitrangda brought to the role an understated strength and allure. It was easy to understand why both these men were besotted with her. Geeta is no pushover. She makes her own decisions. Her compassion is perhaps what enables her to endure hardship and continue to stand.

Kay Kay dialled down his signature intensity to enable Siddharth to be both stubborn and vulnerable. There are scenes in which he looks terrified and out of his depth, which feels exactly right. And yet the rigidity of Siddharth's beliefs makes him the least compelling character of the three. Geeta and Vikram's malleability makes them richer characters. Shiney, all glib talk and smooth moves, is pitched perfectly as the operator who works the system until it engulfs him. It's desperately sad that, as he goes down, he's screaming that the minister is his friend.

In *Hazaaron Khwaishein Aisi*, Sudhir captures a specific moment in Indian history. But the ideas and emotions in the film feel timeless. There is a sense that the rhythms of rebellion and idealism, disillusionment and defeat will be repeated generation after generation. Which is why the film continues to resonate.

You can watch *Hazaaron Khwaishein Aisi* on Netflix.

12

Hum Dil De Chuke Sanam

'*Ab main jaana keh rahi ho kya fasaana / pyar karne se bhi mushqil hai nibhaana*'. These lyrics by Javed Akhtar are from a song I love—'*Gallan Goodiyaan*' from *Dil Dhadakne Do*. As I listened to it for the umpteenth time, I realized that these lines could have served as the tagline for a film I love: Sanjay Leela Bhansali's *Hum Dil De Chuke Sanam*.

HDDCS (as it was popularly called) is swoony, spectacular and also, in parts, downright silly. Some sequences have dated badly—there are scenes set in Italy that now play like unintentional comedy, and the gender politics are muddled. And yet, in it, Sanjay, coming straight off his disastrous debut film *Khamoshi: The Musical*, created a moving ode to the sobering truth that it's easier to fall in love than to uphold it.

This film from 1999 established tropes that we now recognize as the Bhansali signature: the love triangle in which one partner remains necessarily unfulfilled; the exaltation of the ache of this unrequited love; the obsession with lamps, especially chandeliers, which play a key role in the storytelling (here, the lovers Nandini and Sameer first lock eyes while holding the rope of a chandelier). Also, the love for flowing fabric—a scene in which Nandini runs, with her *pallu* flying behind her, mirrors a scene in *Devdas*, which Bhansali would make three years later. In that latter scene, the same actor, Aishwarya Rai Bachchan, now playing Paro, runs desperately through a similarly lush set, the *pallu* of her white sari billowing behind her.

Another Bhansali signature: the spectacular dancing. *HDDCS* had seven choreographers, including Saroj Khan, Vaibhavi Merchant and Sanjay himself (and 'Nimbooda' and 'Dholi Taro Dhol Baaje' are arguably two of Hindi cinema's most gorgeous song sequences; their closest rivals would probably be scenes, again, from *Devdas*). Outstanding music too, here created by Ismail Darbar and the lyricist Mehboob. And above all, a defiantly extravagant vision. Nandini is the daughter of a classical singer but their home resembles a heritage hotel. The members of the family dress immaculately. But it's more than the styling. *HDDCS* underlined Sanjay's striking sense of composition, his refined aesthetic, and his ability to turn a frame into a painting—a scene in which Nandini tries to commit suicide has blood, water, colours, light and shadow (perfectly rendered by cinematographer Anil Mehta). The film revealed that Sanjay revelled in creating his own worlds, which admittedly have a somewhat tenuous connection with reality.

You can see a less opulent version of the same story in the 1983 film *Woh Saat Din*, directed by Bapu, which was also about a woman being forced to marry a man she didn't love but whose husband's devotion and care for her then forced her to reconsider her feelings, and even the very meaning of love. That was the Hindi film debut of Anil Kapoor.

Sanjay sets his story in rural Gujarat, which allows him to play with colours, costumes, rituals, accents and music. The romance between Nandini and Sameer, who arrives asking to learn music from her father, is forbidden and therefore more sensuous. It plays out in secret glances and touches stolen in front of the entire extended family. Sanjay exploits the physical beauty of his leads, Aishwarya and Salman Khan. The spark between them is electric. Aishwarya's green eyes, captured in close-up, brimming with laughter, pain and tears, become a leitmotif in the film.

HDDCS retains its power because the conservative milieu was a camouflage for new ideas. The most successful films of the 1990s—*Hum Aapke Hain Koun . . !*, *Dilwale Dulhania Le Jayenge* and to some extent *Kuch Kuch Hota Hai*—celebrated the Hindu family, religious rituals and festivities. Karva Chauth, a contentious, largely north Indian custom of wives fasting for a long life for their husbands, became cool. Sanjay also panders to this, with the exquisitely picturized song *'Chand Chupa'*. And the film unapologetically fetishizes the *mangalsutra* and *sindoor*. But it also asks us to reconsider our ideas of what masculinity is.

Sanjay presents his view through Vanraj, a soft-spoken, introverted lawyer who finds out, a few days after his wedding, that Nandini loves Sameer, and decides to help her reunite with him. When Vanraj's father taunts him, asking where his *'mardangi'* is, Vanraj responds, *'Kya mardangi aurat ko kamzor maankar uski khushiyon par zabardasti kaaboo karne mein hai? Kya mardangi sachaai se muh chhupane ka doosra naam hai? Kya mardangi uss aurat ke saath rehna hai jiska jism toh aapka ho lekin uska dil, uski aatma, kisi aur ki?'* His father understands his point of view and says, 'I'm proud of you, my son.'

This was a progressive stance for the time. The relationship between Nandini and her two suitors is one of equals. Sameer is a man-child whom she pushes towards seriousness. Despite her cloistered circumstances, it is she who makes the final decision to stay with Vanraj rather than leave him for Sameer (compare this with Simran in *DDLJ*, a largely passive player who is handed over by her father to Raj). Nandini, staggeringly beautiful and spirited, is the spine of her film.

I also like how *HDDCS* humanizes the actors—in one scene, Sameer farts loudly, not once but twice. Nandini laughs and calls him '*hawa ka jhoka*'. (Incidentally, props to Salman. I can't imagine any other romantic hero agreeing to do this scene.)

After *HDDCS*, Sanjay evolved into a bona fide Bollywood auteur; you could identify a Bhansali film in a few frames. His artistic stamp is evident in every movie he's made since. And even when the films weren't good (*Saawariya*, *Guzaarish*), Sanjay's unstinting ambition to create something new remained. He never stopped inventing.

You can watch *HDDCS* on YouTube.

13

In Which Annie Gives It Those Ones

'Lunatic fringe cinema' is how Booker Prize-winning author Arundhati Roy described *In Which Annie Gives it Those Ones*. She would know—she wrote the film, did the production design and played a lead role.

The film, first broadcast in 1989, is set in 1974, in the final week of submissions in a New Delhi architecture school. Annie isn't a woman, as the name would suggest, but a burly, goofy man-child named Anand (played by Arjun Raina) who has spent four years in fifth year. Annie can't graduate because his concepts are so out of the box. He refuses to deliver the sort of beach resort, shopping complex or residential tower that the examining committee is happy to sign off on. Instead, he comes up with what he calls revolutionary ideas. Like, plant fruit trees on either side of the 60,000 miles of railway track in India. Put water hoses on trains and let orchards bloom. The soil will be fertile since people excrete along tracks anyway. The scheme will reverse urban-rural migration, he says.

Unsurprisingly, Annie fails year after year. Meanwhile, his life goes round in often-hilarious circles. He has a pet hen named Sangeeta who, early in the film, wanders out of his room. So at the crack of dawn, half a dozen boys are trying to corral her. Arjun (played by Rituraj) says, 'Sounds like Annie's cock is on the loose again!'

The dialogue is a mix of Hindi, English and Punjabi. A typical exchange goes something like this:

Bigshit: *Pata nahi yaar Annie ka kuch.* I asked him in the bogs and he started giving it those ones.

Radha: What?

Bigshit: *Wahi apne* usual ones about rural-urban nexus and fruit orchards. *Bhai*, I'm just a simple *seedha-saadha* man. *Yeh sab mere palley nahi padta.*

This was not how Hindi cinema sounded back then. We were still five years away from Dev Benegal's *English, August* (1994), which is widely considered the first Indian independent film. *English, August*, starring Rahul Bose and based on Upamanyu Chatterjee's book of the same name, had largely English dialogue (including four-letter words!) and a determinedly irreverent sense of humour. It was a radical departure from the films being made in Mumbai at the time (*Hum Aapke Hain Koun . . !*, *Mohra*, *Raja Babu*). Benegal broke new ground but I would argue that the seeds of anarchy were sown by *In Which Annie Gives It Those Ones*.

The film has singular, laid-back rhythms. There is no melodrama or Bollywood gloss. The students aren't artificially attractive or heroic. They are raw, confused, vulnerable and wonderfully dismissive of authority. Especially Radha, played by Arundhati, the resident bohemian who smokes *beedis* and matches a sari with a hat. Later in the film, you get a glimpse of the fiery polemicist that Arundhati would become: defending her thesis, Radha launches into an impassioned speech about citizens and non-citizens. The bored committee orders dinner.

The film makes pertinent points about how the education factory snuffs out creativity. It also questions prevalent power structures and the function of the architect—in one scene, Radha describes buildings as 'piggy banks'. Director Pradip Krishen and Arundhati are clearly on the side of the students. The villain of the piece is the sadistic principal, played by an icy Roshan Seth. The students call him Yamdoot. Yamdoot often starts his conversations with his students with 'My dear donkey'. He dismisses Radha's work as 'this year's bleeding-heart thesis'.

But the political subtext doesn't disturb the film's chilled-out mood. The vibe is authentic, nostalgic and determinedly fun. Pradip narrates the story with warmth and immense affection. The background score consists of variations of Beatles classics (as the end credits roll, the strains of a flute turn into a lovely rendition of 'Penny Lane') and other songs popular in the '70s. The camera snakes in and out of hostel rooms, classrooms, the canteen and also the police station because, of course, at some point Annie must end up there.

Like students everywhere, these characters smoke incessantly, romance, have sex, play table tennis, cheat and trip up the system, sing songs and rib each other. There is nothing 'sanskari' about them. Which is why it's difficult to imagine that the film was commissioned by Doordarshan. It played on DD once at midnight, where presumably few people saw it. But *In Which Annie Gives it Those Ones* went on to win National Awards—Pradip won for Best Feature Film in English and Arundhati for Best Screenplay. Decades later, the obscure film became an underground favourite. It also attracted attention because one of the students—a minor character—was played by Shah Rukh Khan. This was his feature film debut.

Shah Rukh's character doesn't have enough screen time to warrant a name. He's simply called Senior, and is a fey hostel gossip who appears in four scenes and speaks in two. In 2007, I wrote a book called *King of Bollywood: Shah Rukh Khan and the Seductive World of Indian Cinema*. While working on it, I travelled to Delhi for research and, among others, spoke to Pradip about the making of the film and, specifically, how they came to cast Shah Rukh.

Pradip said he was determined to find new actors and so he approached Delhi's leading theatre company, Theatre Action Group or TAG, which was run by Barry John. At the time, Shah Rukh was a TAG senior. He and other seniors, including Rituraj and Divya Seth, started doing workshops. Eventually, Rituraj played a lead role. Divya got the role of Lakes, a hilariously prim student who always insists she's vastly underprepared but of course is on top of everything (each class has one such annoying person). But Shah Rukh was relegated to the sidelines. Pradip told me, 'In a sense, he was already in the heroic mould and there were no heroes in our film.'

That clumsy awkwardness is precisely what makes *In Which Annie Gives it Those Ones* so charming. You can watch it on YouTube.

14

Kabhi Kabhie

Logic has rarely been requisite in mainstream Hindi cinema. Directors and writers, including the biggest and the best, have disposed of it entirely when it has stood in the way of their storytelling. I remember a conversation I had with writer Abhijat Joshi after a screening of *PK* in 2014 (full disclosure: the film was produced by my husband). I brought up aspects that had seemed unconvincing to me, like the device of the letter that keeps the lovers Jaggu and Sarfaraz apart. The film worked on a larger level, but this critical plot point struck me as far too convenient and highly unlikely.

Abhijat then explained a fundamental truth of showbiz: that if the narrative can transport the viewer in ways that remain largely convincing, most people will gladly forgive the smaller loopholes. In other words, on screen, emotion always trumps logic.

Yash Chopra's *Kabhi Kabhie*, made in 1976, is a fine illustration of this. The story by Pamela Chopra and the screenplay by Sagar Sarhadi defy logic at every turn. Even before the opening titles have ended, the lovers Pooja (Rakhee Gulzar) and Amit (Amitabh Bachchan) have fallen in love and parted. When Pooja's parents arrange a match for her with another man, Vijay (Shashi Kapoor), Amit decides that it's best to sacrifice their love and uphold her parents' wishes. He's a celebrated poet but they assume her mother and father (whom we never meet) won't approve of the match. They don't even try to discuss it with them.

Later in the film, when Pooja and Amit meet (she interviews him on a TV show), she prods him about a muse, a special girl who inspired him to create, knowing full well that it was her. By the climax, the film is in free fall. A headstrong woman named Sweety (Amit's daughter) is being rescued by Pooja's son Vicky (Rishi Kapoor); she likes him but he is actually in love with her stepsister Pinky. Everyone is shouting each other's names as fire engulfs the rows of trees surrounding them. It's almost comical.

And yet, *Kabhi Kabhie* is Yash Chopra's most eloquent ode to love. It's a film infused with heartache and longing. The narrative, which traverses two generations, depicts the many shades of romantic relationships: the comforting companionship that Pooja and Vijay share; the more brash, energetic bond between Pinky (played by Neetu Singh) and Vicky; and the bruising hurt of unfulfilled love, which has scarred Amit for life. He becomes a brooding, bitter man who rarely smiles, but there is dignity in his suffering too.

Yashji had little interest in villains. This film brims with good people grappling nobly with matters of the heart.

This angst is aided by a soundtrack that became an instant classic. The lyrics by the great Sahir Ludhianvi and the music by Khayyam have exquisite depth and poetry—the title song, '*Kabhi Kabhie*', became the romantic anthem of several generations. Shot in Kashmir, the song sequence also has a startling beauty, especially the images of Amit, looking haunted by the loss of his love, striding alone at night, intercut with images of Pooja and Vijay on their wedding night. Vijay gifts his trembling bride a book of poetry—naturally, it's *Kabhi Kabhie* by Amit.

The plot is propelled by these coincidences: Pooja's son is in love with Amit's wife's love child from an earlier relationship; Vijay, an architect, is hired to construct a five-star hotel on property that Amit owns; Amit's daughter develops a crush on Pooja's son who, rather cruelly, strings her along only so he can get Pinky back.

The story is unnecessarily convoluted, but Yashji keeps it moving, smoothing out the rough patches with the help of songs and his galaxy of stars. There is a great pleasure in watching real-life uncle and nephew Shashi and Rishi play father and son. Both possess that pink-skinned Kapoor handsomeness, and their characters revel in a specifically Punjabi *masti*. Shashi, as the gregarious, whisky-swilling Vijay Khanna, is especially good.

I think *Kabhi Kabhie* was among the first Hindi films to present the idea of parents as friends. So Vicky blushingly admits to his father, 'I'm in love, *yaar*.' In another scene, he insists to his mother that they are friends (she agrees, saying, 'Yes, we are friends') and then proceeds to ask her if she liked anyone in college. The scene doesn't further the storyline. It's there only to illustrate their informal, affectionate bond.

Later, when Pinky (who grew up in an adopted home, never knowing her birth parents) leaves to meet her birth mother (who happens to be Amit's wife), it's Vijay who encourages Vicky to go after her, saying, '*Pyar kiya hai to duniya ki had tak uska peecha karo.*' Aditya Chopra repeated this sentiment in *Dilwale Dulhania Le Jayenge*, in which Dharamvir Malhotra

(Anupam Kher) tells his son Raj (Shah Rukh Khan) to chase Simran (Kajol). He says, '*Maine tujhe yeh tuntuna bajane ke liye paida nahi kiya tha . . . ab ja aur iss ghar mein tabhi aana jab bahu tere saath mein hogi.*'

This modernity of thought is also reflected in the character of *Kabhi Kabhie*'s Vijay, a man who graciously accepts that his wife once loved another man. In the film's best-written and best-staged scene, Vijay confronts Amit, saying that he should have told him he had had a relationship with Pooja. To which Amit replies, '*Woh dard, woh kasak, woh khalish, jo humne apne dilon mein basayi hogi, aap uska andaza nahi laga sakte . . . daag daaman pe nahi, dil pe liya hai maine.*' The men speak to each other in the foreground while their wives stand silently, listening in the background. Vijay begins by berating himself and men in general for being callous enough to doubt their partners, and ends by applauding Amit's deep emotion. He says, '*Wah Amit Saab, maan gaye.*'

This scene is followed by Pooja weeping copiously and asking Vijay if he is a man or a god, *devta ya insaan*. He replies, 'My darling, *iss duniya mein aadmi insaan ban jaaye toh bahut badi baat hai.*' It's an overarching world view encapsulated in a single line.

Kabhi Kabhie redefined traditional notions of masculinity—the newly anointed Angry Young Man (*Sholay* and *Deewaar* had come out just the year before) was recast as a lovelorn poet who loses the girl. And the film determinedly celebrates the generosity of spirit that Vijay Khanna exudes.

Kabhi Kabhie also firmly rejects the traditional Hindi film notion that you can only fall in love once (Karan Johar, though an admirer of *Kabhi Kabhie*, was still wedded to this idea in 1998—you might recall Shah Rukh Khan, as the widower Rahul in *Kuch Kuch Hota Hai*, tossing a ball and telling his mother pensively that he won't marry again. '*Hum ek baar jeete*

*hain, ek baar marte hain, shaadi bhi ek baar hoti hai, aur pyar bhi
ek hi baar hota hai,'* he says). Of course, Rahul discovers that
this isn't true: he finds love again with his best friend from
school, Anjali. But twenty-two years earlier, Yashji had more
progressive ideas. There is no mention of this idyllic and
impractical One True Love concept in *Kabhi Kabhie*. Pooja,
Amit and his wife Anjali all find comfort and companionship
the second time around.

All the loving and losing plays out against a decidedly
luxurious backdrop. The affluent aesthetic was Yashji's
cinematic signature. In his biography, *Yash Chopra: Fifty Years
in Indian Cinema*, written by Dr Rachel Dwyer, Yashji stated his
stance frankly. 'It's not a crime to be rich,' he said. 'The upper
classes behave better. For romance and complex emotions, it's
better to appear rich.'

In *Kabhi Kabhie*, the richness is revealed in the large, gaudy
mansions; in Vicky and Pinky's dates, where they go dancing,
swimming and even to a bowling alley; and in the gorgeous
saris and shawls. In one scene, Simi Garewal, playing Pinky's
stepmother, dressed in chiffon and pearls, declares, *'Rasoi mein
dher saare kaam hain,'* which made me smile because she looks
like she's going to an elegant luncheon.

But none of this detracts from the grand emotion of the
film. *Kabhi Kabhie* is melodrama in the best sense of the word.
The great poet Faiz Ahmad Faiz famously wrote, *'Aur bhi
dukh hain zamane mein mohabbat ke siva.'* But *Kabhi Kabhie*
will convince you otherwise. For a fleeting moment, you will
feel that love, with all its accompanying ache, messiness and
complications, is all you need.

You can watch the film on Amazon Prime.

15

Kal Ho Naa Ho

Kal Ho Naa Ho, routinely abbreviated as *KHNH*, is about a man with a terminal illness. From this grim material, director Nikkhil Advani and writer and producer Karan Johar fashion a movie that is many things at once. *KHNH* is a deliciously convoluted love triangle, a dysfunctional family drama, a lesson in the art of living large (taking a cue from another film about a man with a terminal illness: Hrishikesh Mukherjee's *Anand* [1971], which featured that iconic line, '*Zindagi badi honi chahiye, lambi nahi*'), and a big, blowout musical with a fabulous soundtrack by Shankar-Ehsaan-Loy.

The songs, written by Javed Akhtar, are fantastically diverse—from the club number *'It's the Time to Disco'* to the shaadi anthem *'Maahi Ve'*. They seem to have no expiry date, especially the bittersweet, National Award-winning title song *'Kal Ho Naa Ho'*, which gently reminds you, with its haunting melody and lyrics, of your own mortality.

I saw *KHNH* at a preview screening a few days before the film's release on 28 November 2003. Back then, this was a Dharma Productions tradition. Ahead of every new release, Karan's father Yash Johar invited select guests from the industry and the press for screenings at the Adlabs movie theatre in Film City. Outside the theatre, live food counters were set up so that during interval, we could feast on *kebabs*, *tikkas* and other delectable dishes. He was not a host content to offer merely popcorn and *samosas*.

Yashji, who died of cancer in June 2004, only seven months after the film's release, was one of the most loved members of the film industry. These screenings felt like a picnic. There was an air of camaraderie and joy. People genuinely wanted his films to succeed.

I attended this particular one with my husband, Vinod. I remember weeping copiously through the climax, as Shah Rukh Khan, playing Aman, took his time to die. The melodrama, as Nigel Tufnel from *This is Spinal Tap* might say, was dialled up to eleven. Vinod, who prefers the more austere cinema of Bimal Roy, Guru Dutt and V. Shantaram, gave me his hankie, rolled his eyes, and said, 'Your love for all things Shah Rukh Khan will be your downfall as a film critic.'

In my defence, *KHNH* is the pinnacle of what I call the Shah Rukh charm offensive. The actor was at the peak of his prowess both as romantic hero and as ideal family man. Aman is so helpful and good-natured that everyone on the street, from seniors to children, love him. But he is also so noble and large-hearted that he engineers a match between the woman he loves, Naina (played by Preity Zinta), and her best friend Rohit (played by Saif Ali Khan), even though she loves Aman. He makes this sacrifice because he is dying and he loves Naina too much to let her suffer.

KHNH is a mash-up of *Anand* and another Hrishikesh Mukherjee film, *Bawarchi* (1972). Like Rajesh Khanna in *Bawarchi*, Aman also solves the many problems that beset Naina's fractured family, teaching them to laugh and love again. Just to hammer the point home, there are frequent references to him as a *farishta* or angel.

Early in the film, Naina, her mother Jenny (Jaya Bachchan) and her younger siblings are praying. Naina says, 'Dear God, if you're listening, *in andheron mein thodi si roshni le aao, thodi si roshni.*' And on cue, the light goes on in the house across the street and Aman walks into its balcony, wearing only a shirt, in the snow. The next day, it's summer.

Which fits into the fairy-tale textures of the film. Nikkhil and his A-list crew (DOP Anil Mehta, choreographer Farah Khan, production designer Sharmishta Roy, costume designer Manish Malhotra) weren't aiming for realism. *KHNH* is a candy-floss concoction in which the depth comes from the sweeping emotions. The visuals of New York (from the Brooklyn Bridge to hip restaurants and swanky apartments) are determinedly glossy and aspirational—like the characters in the film, we also want to be walking those crowded streets, wearing beautifully tailored jackets.

The colours are eye-popping, especially in the songs *'Pretty Woman'* and *'Kuch Toh Hua Hai'*. New York is clean, happily multicultural and the sun is always shining, except when hearts are about to break. The film also attempts to be formally inventive, with split screens, voiceovers and characters constantly breaking the fourth wall. Especially in the *'Chhe din, ladki in'* sequence, in which Aman helps Rohit snare Naina.

This sequence, like other elements in the film—Naina's best friend Sweetu, who is fat-shamed throughout; the randomly inserted gold digger Camilla; the homophobic Kantaben— hasn't dated well. Kantaben, Rohit's house help, is perennially

paralyzed by the physical intimacy between Rohit and Aman.
She thinks they are partners and this is played for laughs. Because
in a mainstream Hindi film with A-list heroes, this would be
impossible.

It's silly and not funny, but this was Karan's earliest attempt
at bringing same-sex love into Bollywood (he was still five years
away from producing *Dostana*). Kantaben, with her bugged-out
eyes and shaking hands, was an ice-breaker. In her own way,
she helped to get the conversation started.

KHNH is overwrought and obviously manipulative. There
are too many convenient plot twists. But the one thing that
helps one overlook all the soft spots is Shah Rukh Khan: he's
animated, energetic and fabulously weepy. I don't know if
he's cried this much in any other film. And he does it all with
practised panache.

Watch him in the sequence at the train station, in which he
must convince Naina that Rohit loves her by reading from his
diary, except the pages are empty so he starts to reveal his own
feelings for her, pretending that they are Rohit's words. There
is such a desperate longing in his eyes.

In another scene, Rohit and Naina do the salsa while
he watches, god-like, from a balcony above. The strains of
the title song begin. Aman purses his lips and looks into the
distance. Cut to him walking on the Brooklyn Bridge. He
spreads his arms out, in that signature Shah Rukh pose, and
sings, '*Har pal yahan jee bhar jiyo*', because of course, *kal ho naa
ho*. It's irresistible.

You can watch *KHNH* on Netflix and on YouTube.

16

Karan Johar

Karan Johar is Hindi cinema's Renaissance Man—like a chameleon changing colours, he changes roles, moving from film director to producer to TV show host to actor to fashion maven to author to arbiter of Bollywood's pecking order to single parent. He has flashiness but also fluidity, which enables him to be all things to all people. His critics dismiss him as a lightweight filmmaker who dazzles with stars and glittering surfaces rather than with depth. But underneath the decorative exterior lies an artist with a keen eye for beauty. Karan has always been unapologetic about who he is and what his cinema is about. Which is perhaps why the gossamer consumerist fantasies he creates attract fans around the globe—including in non-traditional Bollywood markets like Germany and Poland.

I first interviewed Karan in 2001, just before the release of his second film, *Kabhi Khushi Kabhie Gham* . . . He was twenty-nine, and at the time, *K3G* (as it was popularly called) was the most expensive film ever made in India. He told me then that he 'went demented spending money'. Karan's father, the late Yash Johar, had originally set a Rs 25 crore budget for the film. But when the cost of the first song, *'Bole Chudiyan'*, came in at Rs 3 crore, he stopped calculating. In this film, the diamantes are Swarovski, the shawls are Jamevar, the chandeliers are custom-made and the dancers—in *'Say Shava Shava'* at least—are fifty blondes who were flown in from London. This is perhaps the only Hindi film in which locations in the UK are being passed off as New Delhi.

Karan's cinema is permeated with a passion for opulent and expensive things. Even when he tries to slum it, he can't— he laughingly tells the story of directing a short in the four-film anthology *Bombay Talkies* in 2013, in which one of the characters was a beggar. He says he asked his costume designer how many changes she would have, because it never occurred to him that a beggar might not have clothing options. Karan is often accused of having 'affluenza'—his characters suffer in grandiose mansions, wearing designer clothes. Even the minor characters in his films wear more stylish clothing than many of us ever will in life.

The gloss of Karan's cinema makes it easy to dismiss him. So does his omnipresence (at one time, alongside films, a talk show and dance shows, he was also doing a soup commercial) and his penchant for oversharing (among other things, he has spoken about having haemorrhoids, and losing his virginity at twenty-six). Karan enjoys preening for Instagram. His practised pout is at par with Derek's famous Blue Steel pose in *Zoolander*. He admits to being a shopaholic and proudly displays his fashion-forward dress sense, tagging the various designers who custom-make clothes for him. He once told me that he never worries about laundry and dry cleaning because he never wears the same clothes twice. All of which makes it hard to take him seriously as an artist.

But the truth is that through his career, Karan has helped to push the boundaries of Hindi cinema—whether it's by bringing gay characters into the mainstream, even if it was through problematic narratives, like those of *Dostana* and *Kal Ho Naa Ho*. Or by showcasing the female orgasm, as he did in his short in *Lust Stories*—could you imagine an errant vibrator being the stuff of comedy and empowerment in the way he showed it? And then there's his unerring instinct for music—he's helped to create exquisite songs like 'Suraj Hua Maddham', 'Mitwa', 'Iktara' and many more. In a conversation I conducted with him at the London School of Economics in 2017, he said that his impeccable music taste came from only knowing Hindi film music. He said: 'I'm all about Hindi film music. I'm obsessed by it. That's all I ever listen to. I'm meant to know what Beyoncé's new album is or what Adele has sung but I really don't care.' I always tell him that his songs have provided the soundtrack for my life.

Over the years, I've interviewed Karan umpteen times. I enjoy his quick wit, his delicious stories and his lack of delusion. When I chatted with him about *Lust Stories* in 2018, I asked what was the most embarrassing thing that had ever happened to him on a set, and he unleashed on me and the other directors—Anurag Kashyap, Zoya Akhtar and Dibakar Banerjee, who were also in the interview—a story about shooting 'Suraj Hua Maddham' in the Farafra Desert in Egypt. He said one day, during the shoot, he had an upset stomach. The van was too far so he decided to make do behind a limestone structure, but another member of the crew, also struggling with an upset stomach, was already squatting there. His exact words were: 'We both have stared at each other and we both knew we were hiding. He stared at me and I stared at him and we were both in squat position, and I was like, I'm going to die.' This image ruined the song for me a little, but which other director, I wondered, would have volunteered that story?

There is a certain candour to Karan. In the same LSE chat, he said to me that he was living an honest life. 'I love what I do and I do it.' Karan's cinema may not match the pathos of Sanjay Leela Bhansali's work or the precision of Zoya Akhtar's craft. But his flamboyant personality and his signature panache have helped shape our sensibilities and our cinema. I know that my life is infinitely more colourful because he is in it.

17

Karz

Reincarnation is something of a tradition in Indian cinema. Since Kamal Amrohi's *Mahal* in 1949, audiences have accepted that a narrative can continue over two lifetimes— the protagonist returns, usually looking exactly the same, and fulfils the story arc by taking much-needed revenge or finding the love that was denied the first time around. On paper, it's preposterous. But in the movies, it works. The idea that even death can't prevent good from winning over evil remains consistently seductive and satisfying. Think of Bimal Roy's *Madhumati* (1958), Rakesh Roshan's *Karan Arjun* (1995) or Farah Khan's *Om Shanti Om* (2007).

My favourite film in this sub-genre is *Karz* (1980), directed by Subhash Ghai. The film is a rip-off of the Hollywood thriller *The Reincarnation of Peter Proud* (the trailer for the 1975 film begins with 'You have only one life to live, or do you?'). But Ghai and his screenplay writer, Sachin Bhowmick, reworked the R-rated American film (which featured nudity, rape, shades of incest and murder) into a full-blown musical with terrific songs, a love story, comic moments, suspense and a spiritual angle (a Kali *mandir* features prominently throughout). There's also a mother angle (Ravi Verma is reborn as Monty because he must repay '*maa ke doodh ka karz*') and one of Hindi cinema's most memorable bad girls—Kamini, played with just the right amount of class and crazy by Simi Garewal.

The first time we see Kamini, we instantly know she is shady because she's smoking outside the courtroom while a critical judgment is being pronounced on her boyfriend, Ravi. Good girls didn't smoke back then and certainly not at such pivotal moments. We are meant to understand immediately that her love can't be true. Sure enough, within minutes she's made a deal, with a mute don named Sir Judah (played with comical menace by Prem Nath), to marry Ravi and murder him by running him over with his own jeep. All this happens before the opening credits have rolled.

What makes Kamini interesting is that her malevolence is tempered with insecurity and vulnerability. She's elegant and worried about losing her looks. A revenge-seeking Monty, who is no criminal this time but a rich and famous popstar, plays on her vanity. He fakes love and manipulates her. She's flattered by his attention. She is that rare thing—an older woman in a Hindi film who is also a sexual being. Of course, the film mocks her feelings for Monty, but Kamini is presented as a riveting character. She is determined to live the good life and is willing to do whatever it takes to get it. She has personality and more depth than the film's actual heroine, Tina (played by Tina Munim, now Ambani), a cute but silly, shrieking teenager who steals Monty's heart. Why a famous popstar would fall for a schoolgirl, incidentally, is never addressed (it's icky and illegal). They eventually marry, but I can't imagine that the relationship lasted long.

Ghai and Bhowmick tell the story of *Karz* at a propulsive pace, deftly mixing romance, revenge and suspense. The songs, by the duo Laxmikant-Pyarelal, also further the narrative. The film's big set-piece number, '*Om Shanti Om*', is shot on a revolving dance floor shaped like a music record. Monty arrives on stage sitting on a gramophone needle. With disco lights and dozens of background dancers, it's dazzling but also critical to the plot—Monty starts to have visions of his past life during the song.

Even more essential and tightly choreographed is the climactic number, '*Ek Hasina Thi*', in which Monty and Tina re-enact, on stage, Ravi's tragic love story and Kamini's betrayal. Kamini, sitting in the audience, pushed to the edge as it is, begins to visibly unravel. It's a perfectly orchestrated, high-voltage reveal. Interestingly, decades later, Farah Khan and Sriram Raghavan would make films titled *Om Shanti Om* (2007) and *Ek Hasina Thi* (2004) respectively.

Like the plotline, some of *Karz*'s music was also plagiarized. '*Om Shanti Om*' was adapted from '*Om Shanty Om*' by Trinidadian singer Ras Shorty I. The haunting guitar tune that Ravi loves, and which Monty uses to unsettle Kamini further, was lifted from George Benson's '*We As Love*'. Ghai borrowed liberally, but to his credit he used the music to great effect. It helped that Rishi Kapoor (as Monty) could dance as well as he could act. Wearing gold and silver outfits, he combined flamboyance and youthful energy with sentimentality, and was absolutely convincing as a pop music sensation and a man tortured by visions he couldn't understand (thirty-one years later, Rishi's son Ranbir would also play a troubled singer, with aplomb, in Imtiaz Ali's *Rockstar*).

Karz is a rare reincarnation film in which the reborn character is played by a different actor—Ravi Verma is played by Raj Kiran. Monty doesn't resemble Ravi, which makes his investigation more difficult and intriguing.

I developed a fondness for Sir Judah too. We are never told why he's called Sir—has he in fact been knighted by the Queen, or is it because he's just supremely nasty? He has long, painted fingernails and in one scene, we see him in a bathtub, being bathed by two young women. Sir Judah controls his evil empire by tapping out commands, which are then interpreted by his right-hand man, played by Mac Mohan, whom I consider the superstar of sidekicks. Mac Mohan also gets a few killer lines—in one scene, he tells Kamini that Sir Judah wants to know what she is doing with Monty. When she angrily responds with, 'This is my private life,' he casually reminds her, 'Sir Judah *ke chamchon ya chamchion ki koi* private life *nahi hoti.*' It's priceless.

The high drama in the film is heightened by a circling camera, frenzied cutting and mood lighting. Ghai uses all the tools at his disposal to deliver an entertaining and emotional ride.

You can watch *Karz* on YouTube.

18

Kumbalangi Nights

Malayalam cinema was a late-career discovery for me. I used to catch the odd movie at film festivals, but a sustained interest came only after the advent of streaming. OTT platforms brought the best Indian films, with subtitles, into our homes. They made it easy for movie lovers to access stories in languages other than their own. *Kumbalangi Nights* (2019) was an early favourite. It epitomizes, for me, all that is out there, waiting to be discovered.

Kumbalangi Nights is the story of broken men. Four brothers—Saji, Boney, Bobby and Franky—live in a ramshackle home in Kumbalangi, an island village on the outskirts of Kochi. Their home has no door. The entryway is covered by mesh, as though, like their lives, it is destined to remain incomplete. Every corner of their home seems to reverberate with old slights and grudges. The film begins with Franky coming home from boarding school and finding no one there to greet him. He sits down on the couch and finds an eggshell with a cigarette stubbed out in it. These men live in squalor, but what's worse is that they also live in acrimony. Within minutes, Saji and Bobby are physically fighting. Boney sees the brawling from afar and turns away. He wants little to do with his family. Franky says, 'This house is nothing but hell.'

The ugliness of their lives is heightened by the beauty of their surroundings. Kumbalangi is lush and green. The backwaters shimmer beneath diaphanous fishing nets. Through these juxtapositions with beauty, cinematographer Shyju Khalid distils the ache in these lives. There is no varnish here, just an artful rendering of humans struggling against their limitations and circumstances, against the backdrop of nature, flourishing and indifferent.

The script, by Syam Pushkaran, takes us deep into the psyche of each brother. The centrepiece of the film is a sequence that cuts between Saji and Bobby—the first is with a doctor and the second with his girlfriend. Both weep, Bobby quietly, but Saji with such desperation that his snot and tears wet the doctor's shirt. It's like he's expiating years of hurt and pain. In this masterfully constructed sequence, director Madhu C. Narayanan shows us that despite their differences, these men are tied together by something even deeper than blood.

Kumbalangi Nights is an examination of masculinity. Representing the most toxic extreme is Shammy, played by Fahadh Faasil, who is also a co-producer on the film. Shammy runs a hair salon. The first time we see him, he is admiring himself in the mirror. He pats his perfect moustache and declares with pride, 'Raymond, the complete man'. There's something instantly creepy about him: his need for control, his intrusion into the lives of the women he lives with, the way he intimidates the boys who play football outside his house, his horrifically controlling relationship with his wife. Even when he's being affectionate, you can see the fear on her face.

So when Shammy's sister-in-law falls in love with Bobby, we know there will be trouble.

Through these various threads, Madhu and Syam create an exquisitely layered portrait of love and loss, compassion and redemption, and the ways in which toxic masculinity poisons all the lives it touches. While the film focuses on the men and their fractious relationships with each other, the women are equally memorable—starting with Baby, Bobby's girlfriend, who refuses to be cowed down by her brother-in-law Shammy. The acting in the film is uniformly stellar but the standouts are Soubin Shahir as Saji, Anna Ben as Baby, and Fahadh Faasil. Soubin is exquisite as the tormented head of this frayed family. In one of the film's most heartbreaking scenes, he says to his brothers about their mother, who left them to become a nun, that she 'always had the odour of a pain balm'. And only an actor of Fahadh's calibre could have played Shammy with such precise control that the climax doesn't crash the film. It still feels tonally jarring, but it's not as emotionally outlandish as the action on screen.

The memorable soundtrack by Sushin Shyam helps make *Kumbalangi Nights* work like poetry. There is a melancholic lyricism to every frame.

You can watch the film on Amazon Prime.

19

LSD: Love, Sex Aur Dhokha

Traditionally, mainstream Hindi cinema has been happy cinema. The storytelling form, which is defined by music and mashed-up genres, is inherently optimistic. The narrative lacks cynicism. Much of it is designed to work as uplifting, feel-good entertainment. But since the early 2000s, a new generation of filmmakers has consistently tampered with this sunny disposition, telling stories that more accurately reflect the country's realities. One of the finest examples is Dibakar Banerjee.

Dibakar started in a lighter vein, in 2006, with *Khosla Ka Ghosla!*, the story of a retired, middle-class man fighting to get a plot of land back from a crooked property dealer. But even in this wonderfully funny, slice-of-life drama, Dibakar attacked, with skilful precision, the rot within the system and Indian society—a theme he would return to in film after film. By his third outing, one of my favourites, his vision had become much bleaker. *LSD: Love, Sex Aur Dhokha*, made in 2010, is brutal and brilliant.

It's about voyeurism, about our gaze and the pleasure that peeking into other people's lives gives us. The three stories in the film are set up as content from 'DeeBee World Vision', '*aapke* entertainment *ke liye*'. Which indicts the viewers from the first frame—our insatiable desire for titillating content makes us co-creators of the stories that follow. The act of watching makes us guilty. Dibakar adopts the found-footage technique made popular by Hollywood films like *The Blair Witch Project* (1999) and *Paranormal Activity* (2007). The entire film is constructed using footage from cameras that are placed within the plot: in the first story, it's a handycam; in the second, CCTV cameras; and in the third, a spy cam. The images are sometimes grainy, blurry, shaky, too dark. We aren't watching life. We are watching life captured by another camera.

This narrative device distances you from the action but also creates a rising dread—you instinctively know that no good can come of this act of looking. The first story, ironically titled '*Blockbuster Love*', lands the hardest punch. A student filmmaker named Rahul is making a diploma film—the name is apt because he is a passionate devotee of 'Adi Sir' (Aditya Chopra), who was a key architect of Shah Rukh Khan's Rahul–Raj persona. Shah Rukh first played a character named Rahul in *Darr* on which Aditya assisted his father, Yash Chopra. Two years later, Aditya immortalized Shah Rukh as Raj in *Dilwale Dulhania Le Jayenge*. Rahul strenuously imitates his idol. His film, called *Mehandi Laga Ke Rakhna*, also features young lovers, a disapproving father and an ending in which the father lets go of his daughter's hand so she and her boyfriend can live happily ever after. Through the making of the film, Rahul falls in love with his heroine, Shruti. To accommodate her conservative family, he cleverly offers her father the role of the father in the film. Most of the film is shot in their lavish mansion.

This film within a film underlines the gap between the fantasies that Bollywood sells us and the reality we live in. *Mehandi Laga Ke Rakhna* is hilariously bad, but even as we laugh, we know the joke is on us—the consumers of these impossible, air-brushed romances. Dibakar and his co-writer Kanu Behl (who would go on to direct the deeply disturbing *Titli* in 2014) skilfully seed the toxic male aggression in Shruti's family—at one point, her father forces Rahul to insert an item number into the film he is making. It's funny but also unsettling. Naturally, Shruti and Rahul's love story ends differently from *DDLJ* and *Mehandi Laga Ke Rakhna*. The gruesome climax, captured in night vision by Rahul's handycam, creates a chill that extends to the next two stories.

The second story is set in a convenience store by a highway. A young man, Adarsh (the feature debut of Rajkummar Rao), lies and emotionally manipulates one of the salesgirls, Rashmi, into having an affair with him—she doesn't know that it's a trap. Adarsh plans to seduce her, film them having sex and then sell the video to the highest bidder. As his friend puts it, 'Camera *khazane ki chabi hai*'. The conversation between the men will make your skin crawl—at one point, Adarsh's friend says about Rashmi, '*Bhenji* type *hai, jaldi pat jayegi*'.

The third is about a Punjabi popstar named Loki Local, whose fame gives him the freedom to treat women like they're disposable. Loki's most popular song is called '*Tu Nangi Acchi Lagti Hai*' (this was later changed to '*Tu Gandi Acchi Lagti Hai*'). A young woman who is desperate to be in his next music video agrees to conduct the 'century *ka* sting' on him. But the greed of the television channel bosses sours the operation. It's not enough that they have sensational footage, they want enough juicy content to last an entire season. As the cameraman says, '*Desh ko seva nahi*, prime-time entertainment *chahiye.*'

Dibakar never lets us off the hook. At every beat, he forces you to question your complicity in the events that are unfolding. Which is why *LSD: Love, Sex Aur Dhokha* is so uncomfortable to watch. The film was inspired by the infamous MMS scandals and the *Tehelka* sting of the time, but continues to be relevant because voyeurism is in our DNA. Our gaze betrays us.

You can watch the film on Netflix.

20

Luck by Chance

I love movies about the movies. They speak to my passion, not just for cinema but for the artists who make movies. I became a film journalist because I fell in love with Bollywood. When I started out as a rookie in the late 1980s, the Hindi film industry resembled a gaudy, breathtakingly chaotic Wild West. The films were, more often than not, forgettable, but the personalities—flamboyant, outsized, cheerfully eccentric—were not. After I had spent a few months on the Bollywood beat, chasing stars in studios, making appointments via secretaries, chatting with moms on sets (the heroine, her mother and her hairdresser were often the only women on a shoot), I knew I had found my calling. I was besotted, for life, by showbiz and by the men and women who created our celluloid dreams.

One of my favourite movies about movies is Zoya Akhtar's *Luck by Chance*, released in 2009. It's the story of two outsiders who move to Mumbai, chasing the Bollywood dream. Sona Mishra (played by Konkona Sensharma) comes from Kanpur and lands in the office of Pinky Productions, where a greasy-looking producer named Satish Chaudhary (played by Alyy Khan) promises to make her a heroine but also suggests that she should keep meeting him because they should get to know each other better. Vikram Jaisingh (played by Farhan Akhtar) comes from Delhi, after graduating from the Nand Kishore acting school, where he is emphatically taught that commercial cinema needs 'projection' and 'energy'. Briefly, their paths cross. They find solace and a connection in their common pursuit. But showbiz is a difficult, dirty business that inevitably demands a Faustian bargain: your soul in exchange for fame, riches and eternal life—on screen, at least.

Bollywood has always been low-hanging fruit when it comes to comedy. Through the '90s and even the early aughts, the industry was so outlandish that it was almost too easy to make fun of it. But Zoya, who was born and raised in the business, comes from a place of keen observation and compassion. So even though the film showcases the hypocrisy, mediocrity and grime, it never becomes a mean-spirited satire.

One of its most memorable characters is Romy Rolly, an old-school producer, played with great empathy by Rishi Kapoor. Rollyji just wants to make a hit film. He unapologetically chases success instead of excellence. He consults a pandit, wears the requisite rings, does pujas and casts the talent-free star daughter, Nikki. In one of the film's funniest scenes, when the film's writer (played by a wonderfully droll Anurag Kashyap) suggests that the hero commit suicide at the end, Romy shouts, '*Oye* Institute, festival *ke liye nahi bana raha hoon.*' Romy's curly mop and slightly desperate manner make him instantly comic. But Zoya also gives him an unexpectedly moving moment, in which we see him weep because Zafar Khan (Hrithik Roshan), the star he launched and nurtured, won't return his calls. Romy cries and says, '*Koi izzat nahi rahi meri.*'

The other standout is Dimple Kapadia as Neena Walia, the ferocious mother of the spoilt Nikki. Neena used to be a big star and is now determined to orchestrate her daughter's success too. She micromanages every aspect of Nikki's life and doesn't hesitate to tell her that there is a lot of money riding on her waistline. In one scene, Romy describes her as a crocodile in chiffon. Neena, who is always impeccably dressed and accessorized with oversized designer handbags, is vain, manipulative and opportunistic. It would be easy to dislike her, but Zoya is too sophisticated a storyteller to allow us to do that. She shows us the scars beneath Neena's brittle exterior and gives us fleeting glimpses of the compromises, big and small, that Neena has had to make and continues to make, to ensure that she and Nikki stay afloat and centre stage in a brutal business. She is a barracuda because that's the only way she can survive here.

Almost a decade before Kangana Ranaut made nepotism a household word, Zoya was calling it out in *Luck by Chance*. In one scene, a character says, '*Baahar se aanewale ko kaam deta kaun hai?*' In another, Sona is watching Nikki give an interview about how she actually wanted to be a vet but 'when mom said Romy Uncle wants to sign me', she said yes. The dislike and envy are clear on Sona's face—these are opportunities that an outsider would kill for. Ironically, Karan Johar (whom Kangana memorably called the flagbearer of nepotism on his show, *Koffee with Karan*), playing himself in the film, is the one who explains to Zafar how outsiders often break into the business— by grabbing plum roles that star kids have rejected. That's how Shah Rukh Khan bagged *Darr* and *Baazigar*, and Amitabh Bachchan, *Zanjeer*.

Luck by Chance is filled with insightful moments like this, many of which are both funny and bitter: in one, Nikki is trying to touch Romy's feet but she can't bend enough because her dress is too tight. There's also a superbly constructed montage of a slew of heroes rejecting Romy's film, each one finding a polite, self-serving way to say no. Abhishek Bachchan, playing himself, ends it with, 'Dad was asking about you.' But the most heartbreaking is a scene in which Sona tells the oily producer Satish that she deserves a break because she can act. He replies with absolute exasperation: '*Woh kise chahiye?*'

Zoya is too familiar with the spotlight to be dazzled by it. *Luck by Chance* has the depth of an insider's gaze (pay close attention to the title sequence, which captures with dexterity all that happens behind the scenes) and the starkness of the outsider's take. I think of the film as an angsty love letter to Bollywood, one that ends on a note of hope. Because Sona redefines success for herself and for us.

You can watch the film on Amazon Prime.

21

Jio MAMI Mumbai Film Festival

I'm a film festival junkie. I love the frenzy and passion that festivals arouse, the atmosphere charged with excitement around new films about to be discovered, the thrill of sighting stars and directors, and the perverse pleasure of standing in line with strangers because a certain title can't be missed (my record is three hours at the Cannes Film Festival in 2019 for *Once Upon a Time . . . in Hollywood*). Festivals are a celebration of cinema. A movie carnival. When you are in one, it's so consuming that you briefly believe that nothing else matters but film.

Despite this, I was not a devotee of the one closest to home: the Jio MAMI Mumbai Film Festival. The festival has a rich history. It was started in 1997 by stalwarts of Hindi cinema—filmmakers like Hrishikesh Mukherjee, Basu Bhattacharya, Amol Palekar, Ramesh Sippy and Shyam Benegal. Manmohan Shetty, producer and then owner of Adlabs (the biggest film laboratory in Mumbai), Sudhir Nandgaonkar (one of the founding members of Mumbai's oldest film society, Prabhat

Chitra Mandal) and Amit Khanna (lyricist, producer, entrepreneur) played key roles. The idea was to create a film festival run by film professionals.

Over the years, the festival—usually held in October—became a destination for film lovers. Nagesh Kukunoor's *Hyderabad Blues*, which kickstarted the indie film movement in India, broke out at the festival in 1998. In 2013, there was Nagraj Manjule's remarkable *Fandry*. Oliver Stone visited in 2010, and Zhang Yimou in 2012. Costa-Gavras, Leos Carax and Asghar Farhadi also came. MAMI, as it is popularly known because it is organized by the Mumbai Academy of Moving Image (a non-profit trust), was flourishing. But the festival was held largely in south Mumbai, a one-hour drive each way, which was difficult to negotiate. Ironically, I flew to festivals around the world but ended up rarely going to the one in my backyard.

That changed in 2014. MAMI is almost entirely privately funded, which makes it wholly dependent on corporate sponsors. That year, Anil Ambani's Reliance Entertainment, which had supported the festival for five years, decided not to renew the contract. MAMI had no corpus to fall back on. The festival was scheduled to be held from 14 to 21 October, but until late August, no new sponsors had been found and a shutdown seemed imminent. On 29 August, an article titled 'Mumbai's Rs 5 Crore shame: Who will pay for a film festival?' was published on the website Sify Movies. It was written by IANS journalist Satyen K. Bordoloi. The article went viral, travelling widely on Twitter, which is where I saw it. My first thought was, we can't let this happen. The film capital of the country can't be devoid of a film festival.

Over the next few weeks, I became a film activist. I reached out to friends and strangers to beg for money for the festival. My husband Vinod donated money and also bullied others into

opening their wallets. A builder friend who has nothing to do
with the movies wrote a cheque. As did industrialist Anand
Mahindra, producer Manish Mundra, actors Aamir Khan and
Sonam Kapoor, Lionsgate Studio, and hundreds of MAMI
lovers who donated what they could. The hashtags #SaveMAMI
and #SaveMFF trended on Twitter. The outpouring of support
was overwhelming. In four weeks, we managed to raise enough
money to hold the festival.

MAMI was essentially quicksand—after raising money, I
got sucked into planning the execution of the event. I roped
in my producer Smriti Kiran and associate Kalpana Nair, who
had already worked with me on several projects including the
popular Star World show, *The Front Row*. We worked closely
with then festival director Srinivasan Narayanan and his team.
Opening night at Chandan Cinema in suburban Mumbai was
especially anxiety-inducing. The stage was so narrow that I was
concerned that one of our esteemed guests—Helen, who got
the lifetime achievement award, or Aishwarya Rai Bachchan
or the formidable Catherine Deneuve—might topple off it.
Earlier that evening, Vinod's production people were called in
to clean up the bathrooms of the forty-year-old theatre. We
were petrified that Deneuve might want to freshen up.

The week was filled with highs and lows. I remember one
day, all of us danced, for no good reason, at a PVR theatre, to
Pharrell Williams's *Happy*. Closing night felt like a physical
load had been taken off my chest. Fittingly, the logo of the
festival that year was a phoenix.

In December that year, a board meeting was held and the
management of the festival was officially handed over to us—
filmmaker Kiran Rao became chairperson; I, festival director;
and Smriti, creative director. The titles were impressive but we
had inherited a leaking ship: MAMI came to us with a skeletal
team and a debt of Rs 75 lakh. Over the next six months,

we scrambled to find money. Smriti, Kiran and I became salespeople, travelling from one corporate office to another, hoping to convince brands to sign on. We were often asked: what is the ROI? We didn't even know at first that ROI meant return on investment.

How do you measure the ROI of a film festival? What price tag can you put on an event that fosters creativity, shapes mindsets and nurtures the next generation of storytellers? In India, a festival becomes even more valuable because most of the films shown (complex, layered and difficult to market) are unlikely to get a commercial release. Viewers might be able to access some of them on streaming platforms but the festival becomes the only space for a big-screen experience of these movies. Most importantly, a festival gives viewers a chance to watch films uncensored. The image is received exactly as the director intended it to be, untainted by smoking warnings and bleeps, untouched by cuts. In India, this is an unimaginable luxury.

Thankfully, two entertainment behemoths, Star India and Jio, saw value in MAMI. Star signed on first, in February 2015. Kiran, Smriti and I were at the Berlin Film Festival, huddled in a shuttle van, when the call came from Gayatri Yadav, then executive vice president for marketing and communications at Star India. She gave us the happy news that Star was on board as associate sponsor. In June that year, Jio came on board as principal sponsor, with Nita Ambani joining as co-chairperson and Isha Ambani joining the MAMI board. We had found the anchors the festival so desperately needed.

MAMI was the first time, to paraphrase the words of Theodore Roosevelt, I 'dared greatly'. It was the first time, professionally, I had the privilege of building something from the ground up. We reconstructed the festival brick by brick and experienced both spectacular failure (no one showed up to one of my favourite initiatives, open-air screenings for the public) and exhilarating success (the 2015 opening ceremony was at the Gateway of India and the 2016 opening at the newly renovated Royal Opera House).

We learned to choose our battles wisely, deflect criticism with grace and accept that there were things we simply couldn't control. I understood then that to work at a film festival is to be a career diplomat. 'Please' and 'Sorry' became a consistent part of my vocabulary.

I don't consider myself a professional festival person. I am, by instinct, a film critic and a journalist. But I see my work at MAMI as a way to give back to cinema and to the film industry. It's a privilege to have the opportunity.

22

Maqbool

'Kya sab gunah tha, miyan?' This question comes towards the end of *Maqbool*, Vishal Bhardwaj's riveting interpretation of Shakespeare's *Macbeth*. Nimmi, dying from the ravages of childbirth in Maqbool's arms, is weeping and almost pleading with him to tell her that their bond wasn't tainted by the blood they spilt. *'Humara ishq toh paak tha,'* she says. He doesn't answer but holds her and heaves with sobs. It's too late. Their relationship has upended the order of their world. And they must pay for their transgressions.

Macbeth is an epic tragedy about ambition and greed, crime and punishment. By setting it in the Mumbai underworld, Vishal alters the stakes. Unlike in the play, the characters in the film aren't kings or nobles or generals. They're criminals who spill blood every day without hesitation or remorse. In this violence-steeped environment, how can one more murder, even if it is of a father figure, lead to a crisis of conscience? And yet, this is precisely what Vishal depicts with dexterity and empathy.

Maqbool is a doomed love story, a *Godfather*-like crime saga and a gripping character study, all in one.

Vishal constructs a precisely defined world. This is, as Kaka (the Banquo figure) says, a *'chhota sa parivaar.'* And the family, like the locality they live in and the state, is ruled by Jahangir Khan, respectfully addressed as Abbaji. Like Don Corleone in *The Godfather*, Abbaji is a benevolent dictator. He exudes power. We never see him kill but we understand that this is a man capable of extreme brutality.

In one scene, he merely force-feeds *paan* to a man who has slighted him, but it's chilling. Pankaj Kapur, raspy and paunchy, plays the many moods of Abbaji with aplomb. He is childlike in his love for Nimmi, even kissing her feet when she gets hurt, but that doesn't stop him from lusting after a younger woman. His desire feels almost grotesque, and yet this is a man also capable of great affection. There are scenes in which he holds Maqbool like a child and comforts him. Abbaji trusts Maqbool as a father would trust his son. His daughter's engagement is held in Maqbool's house, which Abbaji describes as safe as a mother's womb. Ironically, it is there that he is murdered.

Unlike Lady Macbeth, Nimmi isn't Maqbool's wife. She's his boss's consort. Maqbool was raised in Abbaji's home. If Abbaji is the paternal force, that makes Nimmi, at least obliquely, a maternal figure (even though Nimmi and Maqbool are closer in age, think about the Freudian implications of that). Their union violates the laws of the world they inhabit. In keeping with the brutal nature of this world, they must break more of its laws and spill the blood of one of their own, or give up on the life they yearn for. This isn't murder for murder and ambition alone; it's murder most foul for a throne and a heart. There is an unseasonal storm on the night Maqbool murders Abbaji. Even the heavens seem to roil over what Nimmi and Maqbool have done. You know there can be no happy ending for them; you'd know it even if you'd never heard of *Macbeth*.

Nimmi is one of Hindi cinema's most beguiling heroines. She's manipulative and reckless. Desperate for love, but selfish. She acts without considering the consequences, and through it all there is such vivacity to her. The layers and sexual tension are helped by Irrfan and Tabu's electric chemistry—in one scene, Nimmi deliberately steps on a thorn so that he will have to bathe her foot and she can lean on him as they walk.

She wants Maqbool so desperately that as she goads him into killing their master, she says with unsettling clarity, '*Kisi ek ko marna hoga, hum ya Jahangir.*' Maqbool—conflicted but powerful as Abbaji's lieutenant and yet vulnerable and insecure about his position in this criminal kingdom—succumbs.

This is one of Irrfan's most nuanced performances. With his hooded eyes and understated expression, he imbues Maqbool with dignity. Incredibly, he even manages to capture something childlike in this man who kills for a living—when Nimmi flirts with him in front of others, he seems shy and bewildered.

The seasoned cast enables us to find the humanity in these troubling characters. The screenplay, by Vishal Bhardwaj and Abbas Tyrewala, situates them more often in familial surroundings than in criminal ones. So we see them eat and drink together, celebrate an engagement with song and dance (Maqbool even cooks and chops vegetables for the feast), go to the *dargah* together—it's a typical extended Indian family, except this is the mob.

Vishal's masterstroke was casting Naseeruddin Shah and Om Puri as the witches: they play Inspector Purohit and Inspector Pandit respectively, corrupt police officers who are on Abbaji's payroll. Pandit creates astrological charts and predicts the future. Their jovial subservience hides their Machiavellian scheming—they tweak and twist the finely maintained balance of power, the *santulan* or symmetry of their universe.

The film begins with a close-up of a chart that Pandit is drawing with one finger on the fogged-up window of a police van. The inclusion of these two adds an element of timelessness to the film, a sense that these games of power, greed, love and death have been playing out since the world began.

Maqbool released in 2003, a year in which the biggest hits were *Koi . . . Mil Gaya*, *Kal Ho Naa Ho* and *Chalte Chalte*. I first saw the film in the editing suite in Vishal's office. Even this less-than-ideal viewing environment did not detract from the power of the storytelling. It was my favourite film of the year. And it continues to haunt with its operatic tragedy.

You can watch *Maqbool* on Disney+ Hotstar and on YouTube.

23

Monsoon Wedding

Weddings and movies are a match made in heaven, especially in India. The song, dance, spectacle, colour and inherent drama built into our marriage functions, where families, not individuals, are uniting until death do them part, is tailor-made for cinema. Which is why generations of directors have returned again and again to the wedding trope.

The original specialist was Yash Chopra. He was Hindi cinema's high priest of romance, and the *shaadi* sequence allowed him to showcase the elements that were closest to his heart: love, ache, beautiful men and women in beautiful clothes, a certain upper-class splendour and energetic (sometimes Punjabi folk) songs. To see a master at work, watch the tender title sequence in *Kabhi Kabhie*, in which Pooja is marrying a man she doesn't love; or the friend's wedding in *Silsila*, where Amit and Chandni meet and flirt in song; or the gorgeous '*Mere Haathon Mein Nau Nau Choodiyan Hain*' sequence in *Chandni*, in which she dances up a storm while Rohit obsessively takes photos of her.

Sooraj Barjatya went a step further with *Hum Aapke Hain Koun . . !*, a film so deeply embedded in wedding rituals that it earned the descriptor 'wedding video'. Aditya Chopra carried forward his father's legacy with *Dilwale Dulhania Le Jayenge* (in which the whole second half revolved around Simran's *shaadi*) and subsequent productions like *Band Baaja Baaraat*, the love story of two wedding planners. Karan Johar took *shaadi* extravagance a notch higher with his films. The costumes got more blingy and the song sequences more elaborate: think of *'Saajanji Ghar Aaye'* in his first film *Kuch Kuch Hota Hai*, or *'Maahi Ve'* in *Kal Ho Naa Ho*.

In 2019, creators Zoya Akhtar and Reema Kagti took the *Band Baaja Baaraat* wedding-planner theme further with *Made in Heaven*, a multi-season web-streaming series revolving around weddings and told through the lives of two wedding planners. The consistent sumptuous showcasing of weddings onscreen seeped into the real world—choreographed family dances became de rigueur. I remember a showbiz wedding during which guests had to sit through several painstakingly rehearsed but awkward dances performed by the bride's and groom's relatives. When Karan rolled his eyes, I smiled and said to him, 'You started it, now you suffer it.'

You could argue that the Indian *shaadi* film constitutes its own genre, but there is one film that stands apart from the rest: Mira Nair's marvellous *Monsoon Wedding* (2001). For starters, the film, shot in a month on a low budget (approximately $1.5 million), mostly using hand-held cameras, with an ensemble cast of sixty-seven, has a documentary feel to it. The film takes place over four days as relatives gather for an arranged wedding in an upper-middle-class Delhi home. There are complications: the bride is still longing for her married lover; long-simmering resentments come to the fore; as various ceremonies and rituals take place, other love stories start to blossom; and eventually, a dark, disturbing family secret is unveiled.

Mira Nair infuses writer Sabrina Dhawan's script with an intoxicating Punjabi *masti*. The film celebrates the chaos and confusion that a wedding brings with it: gifts have to be bought, bills paid, family politics handled and nerves calmed. At the centre of it all is the hapless father of the bride, Lalit Verma (one of Naseeruddin Shah's finest performances). The film begins with him berating the wedding planner because the work is so shoddy. This mix of irritation, frustration and sadness at his daughter's leaving is Lalit's permanent mood. In one of the film's finest scenes, he gazes upon his sleeping daughter and niece and says, 'Sometimes when I look at them, I feel love which I almost cannot bear.'

The other unforgettable character is the wedding arranger, P.K. Dubey, played by Vijay Raaz. Dubey, rail-thin in safari suits and dark glasses, is the king of *jugaad*. He is constantly hustling, insisting to Lalit that '*aapki bitiya, hamari bitiya*', and that he is doing 'foreign-style *mein saara kaam*'. Dubey finishes sentences with the comically contradictory phrase 'exactly and approximately', which captures beautifully his way of life and business—and the truth of planning a wedding itself.

Dubey is a smooth operator, but this wedding proves to be his undoing because he falls in love with Alice, played by a radiant Tillotama Shome. Alice works in the Verma home and the romance between them plays out with a sweetness that will make you swoon. Dubey, a gruff, constantly cussing man, becomes a lovelorn Devdas. In one scene, he simply sits on the terrace of his home and weeps with longing. It's twilight and the classical song '*Ras Ke Bhare Tore Nain*' plays in the background. It's magic.

The other standout is Shefali Shah (then Shefali Shetty) as Ria, Lalit's niece, who finally decides to speak up. *Monsoon Wedding* is enjoyable because every frame exudes the scent of home. Each character feels familiar—from the uncle who tells

dirty jokes to the flirty cousin. Indians everywhere, irrespective
of religion and geography, have been to a wedding like this
one. And families, no matter where you come from, are
something like this: a necessary support system, an unshakable
responsibility, and sometimes, a prison.

Monsoon Wedding is also a love letter to Delhi. DOP Declan
Quinn captures the beauty of the expansive lawns and roads,
the gullies of Old Delhi where Dubey lives, the crowds, and
of course, the lashing, invigorating rains. The soundtrack by
Mychael Danna, who went on to win an Oscar for his work on
Life of Pi, is exquisite. The film also features a young Randeep
Hooda (it was his first film) and Ram Kapoor. Arjun Bhasin,
who was barely known then, did the costumes; Farah Khan, the
choreography; and the assistant directors included filmmaker
Kiran Rao.

Towards the end of *Monsoon Wedding*, Lalit says, 'My
family means everything to me.' But this film was among the
first to show sexual abuse, to puncture the mirage of the happy
Indian family, and to ask what price we were willing to pay to
keep it together. *Monsoon Wedding* distils, without sanitizing,
the essence of the Indian family. Which is what makes it one
for the ages.

24

Mughal-e-Azam

Romance is a staple of Hindi cinema. No matter what the plot or genre—be it family drama, murder mystery, comedy, horror or superhero saga—at some point, two people will fall in love.

Films in which this doesn't happen are outliers, or in industry parlance, '*hatke*'. Which effectively means that over more than a century of Indian cinema, we've seen millions of romances play out. Boy meets girl has transcended from custom to cliché. And yet I would argue that, despite the advances in technology and storytelling, no film has been able to surpass the exquisite romance of K. Asif's 1960 masterpiece, *Mughal-e-Azam*.

The forbidden love affair between the crown prince of the Mughal empire and a *kaneez*, or slave girl, is a tragedy enhanced by spectacle. Salim and Anarkali (which means pomegranate blossom) aren't mere mortals. Their actions and utterances shape the course of history. It's a testament to Asif's artistry that as we watch, we are so immersed in the sweeping narrative that we forget it's a fabrication. There is no conclusive evidence to suggest that Anarkali existed. Or that Emperor Akbar and his son Salim, who would later ascend the throne as Emperor Jahangir, battled—literally—because Akbar was so incensed that Anarkali might become empress. *Mughal-e-Azam* exerts such power that fiction becomes fact.

For starters, the film stars Madhubala and Dilip Kumar, the Platonic ideals of regal Indian beauty. When we first see her, she is disguised as a statue, covered in white plaster. Both Salim and Akbar marvel at the perfection of the statue but we, the viewers, aren't shown what they can see. When the statue is exposed, we can only guess at the beauty beneath the plaster. But a few scenes later, Asif masterfully unleashes Madhubala in the song *'Mohe Panghat Pe'*. She lifts her veil and bites her lip, flirtatiously, in close-up. Her blouse is dangerously tight and high-cut. *'Mohe Panghat Pe'* is a rare instance of a religious song playing out as seduction. The prince is smitten and so are we.

This love story has frisson because it is doomed. And because it unfolds in gilded chambers and ornate alcoves. Anarkali sends Salim a note embedded in a lotus that floats downstream from her part of the palace to his. Her sister Suraiya acts as go-between. And the Machiavellian Bahar (played with icy cool by Nigar Sultana) is the rival who derails the relationship at every opportunity because she wants the crown for herself.

Early in the film, Bahar sets up a *qawwali* competition between herself and Anarkali, to be judged by Salim. Anarkali and Bahar face off in the memorable song *'Teri Mehfil Mein'*. At the end, the prince decides that Anarkali's stance that love is worth risking ruin for, will only bring her thorns. But Anarkali masterfully sidesteps this ostensible defeat with the immortal line *'Zehnaseeb. Kaanton ko murjhane ka khauf nahi hota.'*

Mughal-e-Azam is filled with mic-drop moments like this one. The dialogue, credited to four writers—Kamal Amrohi, Aman, Ehsan Rizvi and Wajahat Mirza—is so sparkling that generations of viewers have memorized lines. When the colourized version of the film was released in 2009, theatres became like karaoke bars, with viewers saying the lines along with the characters. So when Jodha confronts Akbar, accusing him of being heartless, and he rebukes her saying, '*Aap sirf maa hai, sirf maa*,' the viewers replied before the empress did: '*Aur aap sirf shahenshah hai, sirf shahenshah.*'

Even when no one speaks, the spell *Mughal-e-Azam* casts remains unbroken. In one of the film's finest scenes, Salim and Anarkali meet in a courtyard filled with flowering trees. Blossoms are strewn everywhere. The court musician Tansen, voiced by the legendary Bade Ghulam Ali Khan, sings '*Prem Jogan Ban Ke*' in the background. The prince caresses Anarkali's face with a feather and then leans in for a kiss. Of course we never see lips touch. Just two bodies leaning into each other behind a feather. And yet this is, hands down, the most sensuous love scene in Hindi cinema.

A love story is only as good as the opposition. And can there be a fiercer opponent than an emperor willing to sacrifice his son for the good of the country? Prithviraj Kapoor, stern and solid like a rock wall, is formidable as Akbar. His rage sears the screen, especially in the film's most iconic song, '*Pyar Kiya Toh Darna Kya*'. Originally, this was the only coloured sequence in the film, and it is spectacular. A defiant Anarkali declares her love for Salim—at one point, she kneels in front of him and sings '*Unki tamanna dil mein rahegi, shamma isi mehfil mein rahegi*'—while the emperor looks on, seething. The Sheesh Mahal or Hall of Mirrors echoes, visually and aurally, Anarkali's undying passion. As she forcefully declares, '*Purdah nahi jab koi khuda se, bando se purdah karna kya*', she reduces an emperor to a commoner with her emotion.

But Asif isn't interested in creating villains. That would be too easy. And *Mughal-e-Azam* was his dream project, over which he toiled for two decades. Instead, in Emperor Akbar, Asif creates a giant of a man who is bound by duty and justice. We see his human side—before they fight each other on the battleground, he approaches Salim and attempts to make peace. But the father and son cannot reconcile. Asif also makes a case for love and individual freedom, especially through the character of the sculptor Kumar, who consistently speaks truth to power.

Ultimately, love must be sacrificed for the greater good. But Anarkali has the upper hand morally and the emperor recognizes this—he tells her that the Mughals will remember her favour.

Mughal-e-Azam is the gold standard for the historical in Hindi cinema. Any director who ventures into the territory is instantly compared and found wanting. Sanjay Leela Bhansali is perhaps the only one who has managed to come close to this level of spectacle and operatic emotion. But even he has never had a Madhubala and a Dilip Kumar lighting up the screen together.

Mughal-e-Azam is as much a myth as it is a movie. If possible, find the original black-and-white film. The colourized version, with its gaudy pinks and too-bright blues, taints the elegance of Asif's frames. This story didn't need more visual flamboyance. It is, as it stands, perfect.

25

Nayakan

'*Jaante ho duniya mein sabse bada bojh kya hota hai,*' the elderly Imaam Saheb, whose son Ahmed has been murdered by Gabbar Singh, asks in *Sholay*. '*Baap ke kandhe par bete ka janaza.*' In a single line, writers Salim-Javed encapsulate the anguish of a grieving parent.

In *Nayakan*, director Mani Ratnam and actor Kamal Haasan go a step further. They do away with words. When Velu Naicker lifts the shroud and sees his son's burnt corpse, he lets out a cry so primal that his grief seems to pierce the heavens. In the next scene, Velu leads his son's funeral procession as the rain beats down.

Velu is a powerful but benevolent don who inspires absolute loyalty—at one point, an elderly woman immolates herself to protect him from the police. He leads a lawless life but has a strong moral centre. *Nayakan*, inspired by the story of the real-life Mumbai don Varadarajan Mudaliar, is a masterful study of this contradiction. In the film's climax, Velu's grandson asks him, are you good or bad. Velu says, I don't know.

Nayakan means lord or master in Tamil. Mani Ratnam, who also wrote the story and screenplay, sets up systemic corruption and brutality against an individual who refuses to capitulate. The playing field is skewed in favour of the rich and powerful; in several scenes, we are reminded that no one cares about the lives of the poor. So Velu decides that there is no point in playing by the rules.

We live through his eventful life, we understand the circumstances that make him the man he is; we also see the heavy price he pays. Velu is only a teenager when he first murders a police officer, but the officer had murdered his father, who was a labour union leader. Violence begets violence. And Mani Ratnam asks us to consider afresh how we define right and wrong.

The brilliance of the film is that these weighty questions of good and evil, crime and punishment, are woven seamlessly into a gripping gangster saga. The plot spans several decades, from Velu's wretched childhood to when he is a white-haired man with a noticeable paunch who walks with the authority of a monarch. Velu's smallest gesture can incite riots. We know he is capable of brutality—early in the film, he bludgeons a police officer to death. But he is also emotional and vulnerable. His life is anchored by his relationships with his family and the people of Dharavi, where he lives. Mani Ratnam and Kamal Haasan construct a three-dimensional portrait of a man who cannot be slotted or defined.

Early in the film, we see Velu develop a relationship with Neela (played by debutant Saranya), a prostitute. In one of the film's most tender scenes, she requests him to let her go by 1 a.m. so she can study for her maths exam the next day. He agrees and sleeps on a chair while she crams with her books on the floor.

When Velu first sees Neela, she is partly hidden by a
mosquito net. Later, we see them and their two children
ensconced in a net, his son and daughter sprawled across his
legs. It's as if the net, fragile and diaphanous, is the only oasis
they could build in the terrifying world they inhabit. You know
it cannot last, because he who lives by the gun must die by the
gun. Velu has lived by the teachings of his foster father, who
believed that if breaking the law helps people, it can't be bad.
But crime, even when performed with good intent, cannot pay.
Velu's transgressions come back to haunt him.

Kamal Haasan as Velu delivers one of the great performances
in Indian cinema. His beefy body embodies the don's brute
strength—even when he is made to look older, he doesn't lose
this imposing physicality. But his eyes reveal his helplessness and
hurt. There is a long, beautifully staged scene in which Velu's
daughter Charumati questions his brand of vigilante justice. She
asks him if he thinks he is God, meting out punishment as he
does. Velu tries to reason with her and explain, but she cannot
see beyond the fact that her father is a criminal. Eventually he
loses his temper. He says he will stop when the oppression and
injustice in the world stop; he lists the wrongs he has endured,
including the murder of his wife. His body shakes with fury and
then, in a heartbeat, he is back to cajoling his daughter, trying to
make her see that he has had no choice.

Kamal Haasan gives Velu a humanity and an inborn dignity.
His tragedy has an almost mythic quality to it, so that when he
finally falls, it is as though a colossus has been toppled.

Nayakan has echoes of *The Godfather* (the cross-cutting
between Velu performing Neela's last rites and her murderers
being killed by his men pays homage to the iconic baptism scene
in the American classic) and *Deewaar* (the aforementioned scene
of Velu angrily telling his daughter what he went through is a
throwback to Vijay the smuggler reminding his police officer

brother of all they endured before he turned to crime), but the film is a groundbreaking original.

I first saw *Nayakan* in the early 1990s (the music and storytelling of Mani Ratnam's *Roja*, which was released in 1992, might have compelled me to seek out the director's earlier work). I remember being hypnotized by Kamal Haasan's performance and especially the son's death scene.

Over the years, I came to admire the sophistication and craft of the film. *Nayakan* was released in 1987. At the time, Hindi cinema was dominated by blustering action dramas such as Anil Sharma's *Hukumat* (front-lined by Dharmendra, who mostly just flared his nostrils to convey anger) and Rakesh Roshan's *Khudgarz*, in which Shatrughan Sinha and Jeetendra outdid each other in histrionics. The mainstream Hindi films of that time were designed to be like entertaining morality plays. Good and evil were clearly defined. There was little room for ambiguity or nuance.

Nayakan defies this simplistic duality not just in content but also in technique. Through the film, we see characters positioned in doors and windows, the frame within the frame underlining how circumscribed they are by their destiny. Note the meticulous placement of Ilaiyaraaja's unforgettable music and background score (this was his 400th film), especially the plaintive 'Thenpandi Cheemayile'. Cinematographer P.C. Sreeram and art director Thotta Tharani were also key architects, helping to realize Mani Ratnam's vision of an epic.

Both of them and Kamal Haasan won National Awards for their work on the film. *Nayakan* influenced generations of filmmakers and was featured on *Time* magazine's All-Time 100 Movies list (curated by critic Richard Corliss). Kamal Haasan and Mani Ratnam never worked together again, perhaps fearing anything else they created would pale in the shadow of *Nayakan*.

You can watch the film on Amazon Prime.

26

Priyanka Chopra Jonas

In February 2016, I was at the Munich airport, browsing through the neatly stacked shelves of glossy magazines at the bookstore, when a familiar face caught my eye: Priyanka Chopra Jonas, looking glamorous on the cover of the US edition of *Elle*. She was one of only a few women of colour, and the only Indian, in the several rows of impossibly attractive faces. I remember feeling a rush of pride. Before getting on the plane, I tweeted: 'Bookstore at Munich airport selling #Elle magazine with @priyankachopra on cover. Am irrationally thrilled! #BollywoodZindabad'.

Priyanka is, as her character Sweety says in the 2009 film *Kaminey*, a 'single piece'. She is the architect of a narrative that has no precedent in Indian cinema. Over the years, she has continually expanded her horizons and gone from a triple threat to a multiple threat: she's an actor, a singer, a beauty queen, a producer, an influencer and a philanthropist.

Her journey is remarkable because it includes two ascents—
after winning the Miss World title in 2000, she made the time-
honoured transition into Bollywood. Her parents were doctors
and she had no connections in the business, but she willed
and worked her way into becoming both an A-list star and a
National Award-winning actor. And then, in her early thirties,
when it seemed like her Bollywood career had peaked (like film
industries around the world, Bollywood is notoriously ageist),
Priyanka simply shifted the goalpost. She started over, as a
newbie in Hollywood, and became the first Indian star to build
a successful mainstream career there.

This is not the trajectory heroines in Hindi cinema usually
follow. Bollywood leading ladies inhabit a paradoxical space.
They are an integral part of the fantasy factory. The most
successful are outsized stars who drive box office collections,
have legions of fans and, occasionally, shape narratives before
work on a project begins. Every era has had stellar female actors,
from Nargis, Nutan, Meena Kumari and Madhubala to Hema
Malini and Rekha to Sridevi and Madhuri Dixit to Deepika
Padukone and Alia Bhatt. But they are also, to varying degrees,
second-class citizens, functioning in a deeply patriarchal system.
Bollywood, like film industries everywhere, is run by men.

At the start of my career, I would routinely find myself on sets
where the leading lady, her mother, her hairdresser and I were
the only women in a crew of over 100. None of us questioned
this. The few women in positions of power (mostly actors) used
their clout to further their careers, demanding full-bodied roles
and even propelling films at the box office (*Raja* in 1995 was
acknowledged as a hit engineered by Madhuri Dixit and not by
the hero, Sanjay Kapoor). But I can't recall conversations about
the status of women in the business. In fact, when an actress
became successful enough to sell a film solo (as Madhuri did),
the biggest compliment the industry paid her was calling her

Smriti Kiran

Sitting with Shah Rukh Khan on the streets of Lisbon in 2016. This was for Film Companion's first branded show, *Beneath the Surface*. He was shooting for *Jab Harry Met Sejal*. My producer Smriti Kiran and I flew to the city for twenty-four hours. It was one of the best conversations I've had with him.

With my favourite Diljit Dosanjh! This was our first interview, in 2016. The designer labels and gargantuan fame hadn't kicked in yet. He spoke in Punjabi and I in Hinglish, and somehow, we communicated and formed a connection. Watching him soar has been a great joy.

I interviewed Martin Scorsese at the Marrakech International Film Festival in 2013. It felt like getting an audience with God. We spoke about Satyajit Ray, storytelling and how he still struggles to raise money for his films. I was so grateful to have the opportunity.

Interviewing Mr Bachchan at the stunning Hotel du Cap-Eden-Roc in Antibes. He was at the Cannes Film Festival for *The Great Gatsby*, which opened the festival in 2013.

On the sets of *The Front Row*, a show I anchored on Star World from 2012–14. In the second year, the show was also done in Hindi as *Star Verdict* for Star Plus. Mr Bachchan was my first guest. His Hindi was so *shudh* that there were moments when I barely understood what he was saying. Somehow, I survived!

Smriti Kiran

Interviewing Jessica Chastain at the Oscars Red Carpet in 2013.
What an exhilarating, incredible experience. Afterwards, I attended
the ceremony. Even from the nosebleed seats, it was magic.

Author

With filmmaker Kiran Rao, who was then chairperson of the Jio MAMI Mumbai Film
Festival, and Smriti Kiran, the artistic director. For the first few years of the festival,
the three of us worked tirelessly to raise money, raise the festival's profile and to lobby
for support from the Mumbai film industry. It was incredibly hard but even more
satisfying to rebuild the festival brick by brick.

At the 2016 Jio MAMI Movie Mela, which I hosted alongside former film critic Rajeev Masand. This was a panel on Karan Johar's upcoming film *Ae Dil Hai Mushkil*.

Getting ready to interview Vidya Balan at the Cannes Film Festival in 2013. She was on the Main Competition jury, which was headed by Steven Spielberg.

Author

With Smriti Kiran and Brad Pitt in 2017. Pitt was in Mumbai to promote his latest release *War Machine*. After a MAMI screening of the film, I moderated a conversation with him, director David Michôd and others. Smriti and I tried not to fangirl but a selfie had to be taken!

Smriti Kiran

With Sanjay Leela Bhansali at the Marrakech International Film Festival in 2013. I am a film festival junkie because when you are at one, time seems to stand still. It feels like, for a little while at least, all that matters in the world is film.

Author

At the 2008 Cannes Film Festival. I was on the Un Certain Regard jury and doing a show for NDTV 24x7, which didn't leave much time to eat or sleep. Midway through the festival, I fainted and the paramedics had to be called in. I was still laughing but look at their expressions—priceless!

Author

Interviewing Ritesh Batra in London in 2016. This was just after I'd asked him if he ever thought about what happened to Saajan and Ila, the beloved characters from his 2013 film *The Lunchbox*. He said he didn't know. But in my head, they are in Bhutan, living happily ever after.

Author

Doing my best to look composed for the camera in the bitter cold of the Berlin International Film Festival in 2016. Even my expression seems frozen!

Smriti Kiran

Waiting to interview Steven Spielberg in 2013. That expression suggests that I was probably nervous as hell and memorizing my questions!

the female Amitabh Bachchan. Decades later, this would be repeated when Vidya Balan was nicknamed the Fourth Khan (after Shah Rukh, Salman and Aamir).

The first time I noticed the presence of more women on a film set was in the late '90s, on Mansoor Khan's *Josh*. When I remarked on it, Mansoor shrugged it off with, 'Women are more efficient.' Over the years, the lopsided equations slowly changed. Women continued to join the ranks and even penetrated traditionally male departments such as music and cinematography. The needle moved further when *The Dirty Picture* (2011), anchored by Vidya Balan, became a monster hit. The box office precipitated disruption.

Around the same time, a new generation of actors emerged; women who were unafraid to call out the industry's double standards. In a 2015 interview, Anushka Sharma spoke candidly with me about the unequal pay scales and heroes getting better hotel rooms on outdoor shoots. She said the bias towards male actors was ingrained in the system. 'Today we are talking about it,' she said, 'because the power game has shifted.' And then she added, 'People don't like women with guts in this industry.'

Priyanka, who debuted five years before Anushka, has always been a woman with guts. I first interviewed her in July 2005 for an article I wrote for the *New York Times* about how heroines in Hindi cinema were letting go of the virginal glam-doll image and experimenting. It was titled 'Bollywood's Good Girls Learn to be Bad' and it started with a description of Priyanka's character Sonia in the Abbas-Mustan film *Aitraaz* (2004). Sonia is a manipulative, vindictive woman who sexually harasses her ex-boyfriend (Raj, played by Akshay Kumar) after becoming his boss. In the film's key scene, she tries to undress him, saying, 'Show me you are an animal.' He refuses and walks away. She screams, 'I'm not asking you to leave your wife. I just want a physical relationship. If I don't have an objection, why should you?'

Priyanka told me that she had a difficult time doing this scene. She had prepared for it by studying Sharon Stone in *Basic Instinct*, but she broke down during the shoot in South Africa. Filming was delayed because Abbas-Mustan had to convince her she was only playing a character. Which sounds dramatic, but think of the stakes here—a globally feted beauty queen whose film career has barely begun (*Andaaz* and *The Hero: Love Story of a Spy* were released in 2003) playing a villainous, sexual predator. It was groundbreaking. Back then, perhaps, it was more instinct than strategy, but right from the start, Priyanka has been subverting the system.

Over the years, I interviewed her innumerable times. In July 2016, we met late at the oceanfront JW Marriott hotel. She was on one of her lightning visits to Mumbai. If you look up the interview on YouTube, you can see the fatigue on my face. But she, as usual, was sharp and energetic. We talked about her career exploding in the West, and she shared a defining experience that propelled her. She said, 'I was told at a very young age, *ladkiyan toh* interchangeable *hoti hain. Doosri* heroine *nahi mili toh nayi ladki* launch *kar lenge, kya farak padta hai?* Subconsciously, it really struck me in my head. And looking back retrospectively, I made my career what it is because I had something telling me that I will not be replaceable.'

There have been missteps along the way (her first Hollywood feature, *Baywatch* in 2017, was a clunker) and Priyanka has her share of detractors (an LA agent described her to me as an opportunist). But I think even her harshest critics would agree that Priyanka is distinctive. The path she has forged is unique.

What I admire most is that her ferocious work ethic didn't falter with success. When her ABC show *Quantico* was being shot in the US, she routinely flew back to India on the weekends to complete Hindi projects such as *Jai Gangaajal* and *Bajirao Mastani*. In October 2016, I trailed her for a day in New York for a show called *Beneath the Surface*. We started the interview in her lavish apartment, then drove to the studio where *Quantico* was being shot, where I spent the day watching her work. Post-shoot, we headed to a party being thrown by a magazine (she was on the cover). By the evening, I was exhausted and she still had script readings and the next day's shoot prep to do. This was her normal.

I once asked Priyanka what she had sacrificed to achieve what she had. She said without hesitation, her life. She added that her journey had been very solitary. That changed in 2018, when she married the American singer and actor Nick Jonas, one third of the Jonas Brothers. When we met in 2019 at the Cannes Film Festival, I asked if she was still willing to sacrifice her life. She said she had married a man who works as hard as she does.

Sometime in 2017, rumours that Priyanka would be the next Bond girl began to swirl on the internet. Asked about them, she retorted, 'Forget Bond girl, I want to be the next James Bond.'

Like I said, single piece.

27

Rangeela

I have a distinct memory of watching *Rangeela* at the Eros theatre in 1995. It was a few days before the film's release. The massive single-screen hall was packed with industry folk: distributors, trade magazine editors, exhibitors. I remember that, as I watched the film, I instinctively felt the thrill of the new. I knew that this was a game-changer, that we were in the presence of something exciting and, to steal Rotten Tomatoes terminology, 100 per cent fresh.

After all, until then, no film had ever begun with the heroine dancing on the streets of Mumbai, wearing trendy dresses and leotards that made her at once accessible and aspirational. This was a film that seduced not with its flimsy plot but with its memorable characters and their endearingly eccentric behaviour (Munna, the good-hearted black-marketing *tapori* who attempts to woo the aspiring actress Mili by dressing up in bright yellow pants and shirt, was an instant classic, and so was his line '*Kya chikna ban ke aaya*').

This was a film that worked as both a love letter to the
Hindi film industry and as an affectionate critique of its
outdated mores. As Steven Kapoor, the perfectionist director
making the film *Rangeela* within the film *Rangeela* (meta before
we knew what meta meant), exasperatedly asks, '*Kaise aadmi*
film *banayega iss* country *mein?*' (After the screening, distributor
Shyam Shroff told me that the character was inspired by my
husband Vinod and by Shekhar Kapur.)

Rangeela is a Cinderella story set in showbiz. Mili is a
background dancer whose talent is spotted by star Raj Kamal,
who gives her a break as a leading lady. Writer-director Ram
Gopal Varma weaves this improbable story like a gossamer
fantasy. The primary weapons in his arsenal are songs: the
soundtrack by A.R. Rahman was groundbreaking. The film
begins with the title song, '*Rangeela Re*'—Asha Bhosle's rich,
velvety voice and the peppy rhythms establish the playful tone.
And then there's the dancing: electric, energized, the steps
rendered with military precision.

The first credit in *Rangeela* after the film's title is that of
choreographers Ahmed Khan and Saroj Khan (she did '*Tanha
Tanha*'). Varma did this for a reason. The songs in the film
are set pieces—they don't necessarily take the story forward.
They are standalone highlights, designed to express heightened
emotions but also to excite, exhilarate and titillate the audience.
Leading lady Urmila Matondkar is very much the pouting male
fantasy, her svelte body on full display—in some sequences, the
camera focuses pointedly on her rear (the film was an early sign
of Varma's obsession with female body parts).

But the ogling is held in check by her manner—she is
furiously sexual while dancing but naïve and bubbly when
standing still. Her styling—the film was the start of the Manish
Malhotra phenomenon—is suggestive of the girl next door.
Though, of course, few girls next door, at the time, wore such

eye-popping outfits. And then there's her relationship with
Munna. They squabble like children. She tries to contain his
natural belligerence (he picks fights with everyone). She wants
him to get a steady job. Underneath these constant attempts at
making him a better man is an outsized love.

We know that this scenario is unlikely to endure—an
ambitious, attractive woman like Mili who is also, by the end of
this film, a star, will not stay in love long with a low-prospects
suitor like Munna. If I had to guess what happened to these
characters after the end credits rolled, I would say Munna and
Mili broke up and she ended up in a bitter showbiz marriage
with the debonair Kamalji (Jackie Shroff, suave and stylish as
always) who, after all, had planned to propose to her after the
premiere of their film.

But while Munna and Mili last, it's a lot of fun. Mainly
because Munna is a stellar creation—listen to his lines (written
by Sanjay Chhel and Neeraj Vora). When he takes Mili to a
five-star hotel, he memorably tells the waiter to turn the air-
conditioning in his direction. When talking about his best friend
Pakya, he says, '*Uska* bad luck *hi kharab tha.*' In a wonderfully
tender twist, Munna helps Mili practise her dialogue for her
screen test and then watches, with a broken heart, as she moves
up the showbiz ladder. Aamir Khan finds exactly the right
blend of cocky, combative and loveable for Munna. He's both
annoying and adorable.

Rangeela also works as a snapshot of a specific time in
Bollywood. By the mid-'90s, the reign of the old guard—
personified here by Avtar Gill playing PC, an oily producer who
wears only white—was ending. By October that year, in the real
world, Aditya Chopra's *Dilwale Dulhania Le Jayenge* would hit
screens, ushering in a new sensibility and a new generation of
artists. It was the end of the era when men like PC ran the show
and when heroines came to the sets with their mothers (the

interfering mother of the high-maintenance actress Gulbadan causes Steven Kapoor to cry out in anguish: 'Hollywood *mein* Julia Roberts *ki maa* Steven Spielberg *ko aise bol sakti hai kya?*'). Steven, with his viewfinder hanging around his neck and his pretentions to be Spielberg's rival, is a figure of comedy. But Ramu also uses him to put forth all that frustrates him about the business, from mediocre standards to spoilt stars.

But make no mistake, *Rangeela* is about the romance of movie-making and movie-watching. Varma pays homage to all that he loves about cinema. In the opening credits, each name appears accompanied by a portrait of a cinema legend: lyricist Mehboob is with Dev Anand, A.R. Rahman with Rekha and Ram Gopal Varma flashes alongside a black-and-white photograph of his favourite actor, Sridevi (which made me wonder if each person chose their own icon).

Early in the film, Munna says, '*Apun* public *hai*. Public *kisi ko kuch bhi bol sakta hai. Jiss mein apna paisa vasool nahi uska dabba gul.*'

Rangeela is full *paisa vasool*. You can watch the film on YouTube.

28

Satya

'This film is an attempt on my part to reach out to all those people who took to violence as a means for their living. At the end of it, if even one of them out there looks into himself before he takes out his gun the next time, and understands that the pain he inflicts on others is exactly the same as he would suffer himself, I would consider this effort worthwhile. My tears for Satya are as much as they are for the people whom he killed.'

Ram Gopal Varma ends his 1998 gangster classic with these words. The intentions are noble but I'm not sure the film is an effective deterrent. Yes, most of the 'Bhais' end up face-down, with bullets in their bodies, but while the ride lasts, it looks intoxicating. After watching the film, all you're really thinking about is the hot-blooded charisma of Bhiku Mhatre; the brotherhood between him and his boys Satya, Chander, Mule, Yeda and Kallu Mama; the volatile relationship between Bhiku and his fiery wife Pyaari; and the ultimate gangster party song, *'Goli Maar Bheje Mein'*.

Satya was the first time I saw murderers, extortionists and assorted criminals celebrate their craft with such boisterousness and sweaty abandon. The music by Vishal Bhardwaj, lyrics by Gulzar Saab (consider the street smarts of the line, '*Bheja shor karta hai, bheje ki sunega toh marega Kallu*') and choreography by Ahmed Khan have so much vitality that, for a brief moment, we want to be dancing with these men. 'A merry life and a short one,' as the eighteenth-century Welsh pirate Bartholomew Roberts famously put it, seems suddenly aspirational.

Perhaps Varma wasn't aiming for this emotional connect, but he and his writers, Anurag Kashyap and Saurabh Shukla (who was also excellent as Kallu Mama), certainly accomplished it. Until *Satya*, mainstream cinema had largely presented the Mumbai underworld as a real-life purgatory where good men went astray. So Vijay in *Deewaar* and Kishen in *Parinda* aren't inherently evil. They are forced by circumstances into a life of crime. They are keenly aware that what they are doing is wrong and, invariably, they pay a heavy price for their sins.

In sharp contrast, the characters in *Satya* come with no backstories or extenuating circumstances. When Bhiku asks Satya, '*Kidhar se aaya tu?*' Satya replies, '*Kya farak padta hai?*' He's right; you don't need a resume to become a murderer. The film's triumph is that, despite this, we relate to these characters and invest in them.

Varma, Kashyap and Shukla humanize these men. We wouldn't want to know them in life, but onscreen, they are great company. In his autobiography, *Guns & Thighs: The Story of My Life*, Varma writes, 'You always hear of gangsters only when they either kill or die. But what do they do in between? That was the thought, which eventually resulted in *Satya*.' So we see what these men are like as they go about their jobs: the dirty jokes they crack as they wait for a builder to bring them their extortion money; their peculiar lingo—*game bajana*, item, *ghoda*; their nonchalance about the violence they inflict and suffer. In one scene, they are torturing a man for information about a rival gang; as he hangs in the room, battered and bleeding, they discuss the woman Satya is interested in like high-school kids talking about their latest crush.

These aren't outsized villains with dens and molls. They are ordinary people who happen to be killing for a living. They operate from a nondescript office that could be the office of any small business. On their dates, Satya and his girlfriend Vidya go to the latest Bollywood blockbuster (in this case, J.P. Dutta's 1997 hit, *Border*). Only, Satya carries a gun.

Satya is a cipher. His heavy-lidded eyes give away little. He ends up joining the gang by chance and then rises quickly, as a master strategist. His intelligence serves as the counterweight to Bhiku's raw energy. But he expresses minimal emotion—the only time Satya softens is when he is with Vidya. Actor J.D. Chakravarthy plays him with a poker face. We never get a sense of what Satya is thinking, which makes him feel doubly dangerous. Unlike Bhiku, he doesn't stand out. His brief, blazing life of crime is a testament to the anonymity that Mumbai offers. Vidya is his neighbour but she doesn't discover, until the end, that he's a gangster. In a scene that's both funny and ironic, they both emerge from their one-room tenements at the same time and she asks, '*Aap bhi kaam pe jaa rahe hai?*'

This sense of ordinariness permeates Bhiku's life too. He fights with his wife, plays with his children, gets drunk with his friends. The film works because the actors are strong enough to inhabit these contrasting narratives. Manoj Bajpayee delivers a career-defining performance as Bhiku Mhatre, a man whose emotions are larger than life so he loves and kills with equal ferocity. Bhiku is impulsive, generous, occasionally unhinged, and Manoj aces each note. In the film's most iconic scene, Bhiku stands on the edge of a boulder against the city skyline and asks, 'Mumbai *ka* king *kaun?*' His character is so dazzling that even though we understand the extent of Bhiku's wrongs, we're rooting for him to succeed.

Urmila Matondkar, wearing beautiful handloom saris (styled by Manish Malhotra), is perhaps the one artificial note in the film. Varma makes sure that his frames are adequately grungy—the half-built apartment buildings, seedy bars and tenement housing localities are wholly unvarnished. But Urmila, who is the moral centre in Satya's life, is perfectly put-together, down to the matching jewellery and make-up (in the song *'Tu Mere Paas Bhi Hai'*, there is even a fantasy interlude in which she dresses up as a village belle). It's a dissonant note, but thankfully this doesn't puncture the gritty textures of the film—perhaps because Vidya represents the elusive fantasy of joy that Satya desperately chases but never finds.

The starkness of *Satya* was especially startling because the film was released amid a slew of candy-floss family sagas: Karan Johar's *Kuch Kuch Hota Hai* came out in the same year. Hindi cinema was celebrating designer clothing, foreign locations and Indian values. Watching *Satya* felt like being dunked in ice-water. It was an invigorating call back to reality.

In fact, what was on screen was uncomfortably close to what was happening on the ground. It had been only five years since the Mumbai bomb blasts, and the spectre of Dawood Ibrahim and the mafia loomed over the film industry. In 1997, music baron Gulshan Kumar was shot dead as he emerged from a temple in suburban Mumbai. Extortion threats were commonplace. Many A-list film producers had hired armed bodyguards. It was a dangerous time and Varma successfully translated that danger onto film.

In his book, Varma writes that there was 'no concrete script on the day we started shooting'. 'I went by instinct,' he adds. Clearly, his instincts were sound. *Satya*'s success set in motion a sub-genre of underworld movies, many directed or produced by Varma himself: *Company* (2002), *Ab Tak Chhappan* (2004), *D* (2005) and *Satya 2* (2013), among others. But none matched the visceral power and rawness of that first one.

You can watch *Satya* on YouTube.

29

Super Deluxe

Sex, spirituality, family, fatherhood, marriage, porn, politics, aliens: how much can you fit into one film? Director Thiagarajan Kumararaja obviously never stopped to ask himself that question, because he squeezes all this and more into his vast, sprawling, sumptuous *Super Deluxe*. The 2019 film, with three narrative tracks that collide briefly, defies genre and definition. It veers from darkly funny to tragic to absurd in a heartbeat. Each frame bursts with colour and meaning. There are perhaps too many things that the film wants to say, but above all, *Super Deluxe* makes an eloquent plea for compassion and acceptance. Like life itself, it is both messy and magical.

Even before the opening titles are over, we are thrust into an adulterous affair, playing out in lurid splendour. Vaembu (Samantha Prabhu who was then credited as Samantha Akkineni) is in bed with her college boyfriend. Her husband Mugil (a wonderfully seething Fahadh Faasil) is at acting class. Somewhere else in the city, three school friends are skipping

115

school to buy porn. And a little boy named Rasukutty waits for his father, whom he hasn't seen for more than seven years, to come home. These stories twist and turn and eventually intersect. There is an attempted matricide, a dead body that must be disposed of; there's also blackmail, a dreaded gangster, a vile policeman, and anguished wrestling with belief and doubt. Is there a God? How does the universe dole out reward and punishment? What constitutes sin?

The writing by Thiagarajan, with additional work by Nalan Kumarasamy, Mysskin and Sekar Neelan, is brilliant. The screenplay stitches the three tracks together, moving back and forth in time. There are some savagely funny scenes: at one point, Mugil is ranting about the dismal state of his marriage to his wife's lover, who is now dead and sitting in the back of the car. Mugil tells him that Vaembu correctly guessed the password for his phone, but she doesn't know what her husband likes to eat! Mugil also frequently rants about the state of the nation. In another scene, he says that he's going to be an actor, after which he'll enter politics because that's where the real acting is.

The beating heart of *Super Deluxe* is the character of Manickam, once a married man, now a transwoman named Shilpa. Other characters derisively refer to Shilpa as 'it'. But Shilpa has beauty, dignity and brute strength when it's needed. When she curses a cruel and corrupt sub-inspector at the police station, several men can't hold her back. Vijay Sethupathi plays Shilpa with deep empathy. There is nothing flashy or falsely feminine about him; he gives Shilpa a certain majesty. Shilpa's existence is itself an act of disruption. She is, in a sense, an artist who redefines and recreates her own identity.

You see the same regality in Leela, played by the beauteous Ramya Krishnan. Leela used to be an actor. She started out doing porn. But she refuses to be embarrassed by it. She says it was just a job, like anything else. Her intelligence and calm force you to forego any quick judgements. *Super Deluxe* prods us to think about the big questions, but even as the events on screen become more outlandish (I did mention aliens in the first paragraph), the film doesn't slip into silly, esoteric or anything less than supremely entertaining. Thiagarajan exerts a tight grip on the unruly plot and finds a place for everything—including 3D porn and Bappi Lahiri's iconic 1982 song, *'I Am a Disco Dancer'*.

Thiagarajan has a keen eye for detail and composition. The colour blue permeates the film—from Shilpa's sari to the priest Arputham's shrine to the tsunami god to the pillars in Vaembu and Mugil's home. In one scene, the characters talking are out of focus but you see ants crawling up a blue pillar. There is life pushing, pulsating, everywhere.

In another scene, Rasukutty (played by a terrific Ashwanth Ashokkumar) asks Shilpa: now that you are a woman, do I call you mom or dad? Which is just one of the many mysteries of life that *Super Deluxe* celebrates.

You can watch the film on Netflix.

30

The Cinema Travellers

Six minutes into *The Cinema Travellers*, I was already crying. The documentary by Shirley Abraham and Amit Madheshiya begins with the projectionist of a travelling theatre, somewhere in rural Maharashtra, readying for the show. There is a religious festival being celebrated outside. The audience is pushing to buy tickets. The reels are delayed. Arguments break out as viewers grow restless. When the spools finally arrive, the ritual *agarbatti* is lit and a coconut broken. And then the magic unfurls. You see close-ups of faces, turned to the screen, filled with awe, joy, sorrow, rapture. It's not entertainment. It's worship.

The Cinema Travellers (2016) is about the power of cinema, but it's also an elegiac, melancholy ode to a dying way of life. India is a severely under-screened country with only about 9,600 theatres, which averages eight screens per million people (in the US, it's 126 screens per million). For decades, touring cinemas have taken films to villages that have no other means of accessing them, setting up like circuses for a few days and bringing colourful fantasies to hundreds of viewers who will have no more movies until these travelling talkies return.

Shirley and Amit follow three men, Mohammed (who runs Sumedh Touring Talkies), Bapu (who runs Akshay Touring Talkies) and Prakash, who has been fascinated by film since he was a little boy and has spent most of his life fixing projectors. These are the last warriors in a war that has already been lost. Film, that is, nitrate film, which needs to be spooled on a projector, is becoming obsolete. Producers have long moved on to digital technologies. The travelling talkies' lumbering projectors, being hauled from one location to another, seem like dinosaurs, and the heavy cans of film an unnecessary load. Even the villagers, in some parts, have TV sets in their homes and demand better image and sound, and the latest hits.

The romance of film on film might be over but the lure of storytelling endures. Their margins are so slim that they can't afford to upgrade but they carry on, fighting the good fight. Prakash has custom-built a projector, which he has named after himself (the name aptly means light). He says, 'I have big dreams.' But there are no takers for these dreams because the business has irrevocably changed. Prakash sits alone in his shop, surrounded by projectors that have been abandoned by their owners. In one scene, Mohammed tears up because he has no money to send his family. Bapu, who says he is addicted to running the cinema, sleeps by his decrepit touring truck and refuses to sell it. Seasonal rain accelerates the decline, soaking tents, making them harder to hoist, turning the ground into sludge and destroying spools of film. Prakash holds up the ruined reels and asks, 'Where are those images now?'

Amit, who was DOP on the film, has a keen eye for detail. His camera finds the small moments, like Bapu using a piece of film to secure the door of his touring truck, or the lone tear that trickles down the face of a young boy watching a movie, or towards the end, in the dismantling of a projector sold as junk, when he shows us close-ups of the tools that will tear it apart. It's heartbreaking, like watching a loved one die. But Shirley and Amit also find the humour in the story—at one point, when the situation seems particularly grim, soft porn comes to the rescue in the form of a film called *Khubsoorat Naukrani*, which has the memorable tagline: 'Not everybody finds one!'

The Cinema Travellers is beautifully constructed. Each strikingly composed frame is steeped in a grand love for the movies. This is a story filled with ache but no drama. For me, the most moving figure is Prakash. I think, if he had been born in another time and place, he could have been a significant contributor to the world of entertainment. At one point, he says, 'Breakdown and repair is the rule of nature. As one creates, another must destroy for the world to function. Once broken, how must it be mended? In that pursuit are born creators. It does not matter that I made this projector. What matters is I created a new thing. After all, life is not just a game of machines but of the imagination.'

There is a haunting intimacy about *The Cinema Travellers*, almost as though Shirley and Amit captured the last flickering of a dying light. Watching the documentary is a bittersweet but essential journey.

31

Theatres

Awake in the Dark is the title of a collection of reviews, interviews and essays by Pulitzer Prize-winning film critic Roger Ebert. The phrase captures precisely what we do. I've spent what amounts to years of my life, awake in the dark.

My association with this peculiar kind of darkness started in cavernous single-screen theatres. India's first multiplex, PVR Anupam in New Delhi, only opened in 1997 (with Shah Rukh Khan's *Yes Boss*). My generation grew up watching films in large, vaulted cinema halls that had eight hundred to a thousand seats.

When I was a student at St Xavier's College, our regular haunts were beautiful Art Deco structures like the Metro and Regal cinemas in south Mumbai. Inside these, there were ornate pillars and marble statues; wide, winding stairways; gilt-edged curtains. But each single-screen theatre had its own identity. Some were grungy and showed A-rated films. Others were cheap, with good snacks, some broken seats and always a few hits running (I remember a rat brushing against my feet at Chandan cinema. I watched the rest of the film with my feet off the ground). And then there were the ones considered a bit snooty, like Sterling and New Excelsior, which almost exclusively screened Hollywood films, and had chicken mayo rolls for snacks in addition to the usual refried samosas and pale-yellow popcorn in see-through packets.

We took for granted the size of the screen and the company of hundreds of strangers. Irrespective of the quality and subject of the film, there was something inherently joyous in the act of sitting there, with so many other people, in anticipation. There were also the joys of prepping for the movies—scanning newspapers for show timings, picking a theatre, standing in line for tickets and hoping the House Full board wouldn't be rolled out before you got your turn (in which case, you could still resort to the black-market sellers, who plied their trade right there, reselling for sometimes exorbitant sums tickets that they had just bought at the box office themselves).

So much of that experience changed with the multiplexes and online bookings. My first multiplex experience was seeing Shekhar Kapur's *Elizabeth* in 1998 at one such theatre in London. The film was a critical and commercial success but, that evening, there were barely four or five people in the hall. I felt keenly the smallness of the space and the absence of an audience. The film was riveting, but I missed that collective energy. This version of moviegoing seemed a little subdued. Soon enough, multiplex cinema halls, with capacities ranging from seventy-five to about three hundred, became the norm. The plush seats, clean bathrooms and shiny concessionaires, with their pizza by the slice, nachos and multi-flavoured popcorn, proved too seductive, and single screens faded out of our lives. We now went there only when necessary.

But irrespective of the size of the hall, the ritual of going to a theatre never became routine. Travelling in Mumbai traffic to a cinema, settling into your seat to watch the trailers (I hate missing these), putting your phone away to lose yourself in another world, and the excitement as the opening titles started, stayed in place even after decades as a film critic (I don't mention popcorn and samosas because I'm gluten- and dairy-free, so I can rarely relish theatre snacks—I always smuggle in my own!).

Admittedly, there were times when the enthusiasm was higher—perhaps for the latest film of an actor or director I admired or one of those big-budget event movies that make you giddy even before they begin. But I've never gone into a theatre with a bad attitude. I never became cynical about cinema. Week after week, we watched mediocre films, but I never lost my optimism that the next one would be better.

One of my fondest theatre memories is watching *Star Wars: A New Hope* when I was ten. As the opening scroll started, accompanied by John Williams's expansive score, I got goosebumps. I knew little about movies but I instinctively understood that I was watching something special. Thirty-eight years later, sitting next to my teenage daughter, I experienced that same frisson as the opening scroll began in *Star Wars: The Force Awakens*. I instantly got teary because it felt like life had come full-circle—the stories that shaped my childhood were now being experienced by my children.

I wonder if these films would have affected us so profoundly if we hadn't seen them on a big screen. I enjoy the ease with which I can access hundreds of movies on streaming platforms, but there is no substitute for the theatrical experience. Especially in India, where audiences are vocal in their enthusiasm and appreciation. I remember a screening of Salman Khan's *Ek Tha Tiger* (2012) in which I couldn't hear the dialogue because the cheering was so loud. But the ultimate movie-as-karaoke moment was watching *Dilwale Dulhania Le Jayenge* in its twentieth year at Maratha Mandir. Most of the audience had seen the film so many times, they were delivering the dialogue with Raj and Simran, singing along with the songs as loudly as they pleased, and sauntering in and out as they wished. They weren't there for the plot. They were there to partake in the pleasure of hearing a much-loved and familiar story one more time. I admire this distinctly Indian audience behaviour. It's what makes our brand of movie madness so special.

The only voluble Western audiences I've seen are those at the Cannes Film Festival. Booing is a festival tradition, as are standing ovations. The audience, made up of critics, cinephiles and industry folk, can be brutal. When Bong Joon-ho's *Okja* played at the festival in 2017, the audience booed the Netflix logo when it appeared as the film started—France supports the theatrical ecosystem with restrictive streaming laws, and Netflix, which produced *Okja*, has a contentious relationship with the festival.

In India, the opposite happened with Martin Scorsese's *The Irishman*, which played at the Jio MAMI Mumbai Film Festival in 2019. The film, also produced by Netflix, was screened at Regal Cinema, where every seat was packed and the viewers included Ranveer Singh and Deepika Padukone. When the logo appeared, the audience roared its approval. They also applauded the entry of each major actor: Robert De Niro, Al Pacino, Joe Pesci, Harvey Keitel. A Scorsese film became a Salman Khan experience.

Movie theatres are my office and my place of worship. As the *New York Times* film critic Manohla Dargis so eloquently put it in a column published on 19 March 2020: 'So much of my life has been defined by—and literally organized around—watching films in theatres. Moviegoing is who I am.'

Absolutely.

32

Supermen of Malegaon

Malegaon is a small town about 300 kilometres outside Mumbai. It is known for its power looms and its long history of sectarian violence (a river divides the town, with the large Muslim population on one side of it and the Hindus on the other). But in 2008, filmmaker Faiza Ahmad Khan brought the town into the spotlight with something happier—an empathetic, affectionate and insightful documentary called *Supermen of Malegaon*.

The movie is about the town's fledgling film industry. The budgets are negligible (about Rs 50,000 per film) and the cast and crew are self-taught. The man leading the operations is director and producer Shaikh Nasir. Nasir learned the basics while running a video parlour (sort of like Quentin Tarantino did). Showing films got him so interested in the movies that he started making them (after getting some practice with wedding videos). The films Nasir makes are parodies of Bollywood classics, with titles like *Malegaon Ke Sholay*—Nasir calls them 'remix films'. But soon, Nasir's ambitions grow and he decides to take on Hollywood by making Malegaon's first superhero movie, *Malegaon Ka Superman*. Faiza's documentary follows the making of this film.

Nasir is making a spoof, so he casts the most unlikely Superman he can find—a remarkably skinny loom worker named Shafique Shaikh whose hollowed-out cheeks and sweet smile make him an instantly comic saviour. When Shafique wears the locally stitched Superman costume of a blue bodysuit, red boxer shorts, red socks and chappals, he looks even funnier. And then there's the actual shoot—*Malegaon Ka Superman* is shot on a video camera and the effects are achieved with croma. So a green screen is attached to the side of a truck and Shafique is hoisted on a narrow bar attached to the truck, so that he's off the ground. He then holds his arms forward in Superman pose, to make out like he's flying. It's the ultimate in DIY filmmaking.

But Faiza doesn't want us to laugh at these men or the decidedly awful film they are making (at one point, Superman pushes against a bus and falls into a gutter). Instead, she reveals to us their passion for cinema, their ambition to create something worthwhile (Nasir wants to make people laugh because, he says, '*hansee anmol hai*'), and their struggle to succeed. Even the most threadbare film requires physically gruelling work and this motley group is also fighting gargantuan odds. At one point, the only camera they have falls into water and Nasir has to travel to Mumbai to get it fixed. But he stays stoic in the face of disaster: '*Aur bahut museebat aayegi.*' Local media cover the film but call the lead Spiderman. The shoot is then interrupted because Shafique gets married.

But Nasir and his team persist. No one here has the luxury of a single job—everyone doubles up. So Shafique is both hero and handyman on set, doing odd jobs. The writer, Akram Khan, shaves his head, wears black from head to toe and becomes the villain. Compromises are made because they can't get the right location. The leading lady has to come from a nearby town because women in Malegaon typically don't work outside the home. When Faiza asks, what if a woman wants to get a job, the reply is: 'She should work at home. What is bigger for a woman than that?'

Supermen of Malegaon doesn't ignore the harsh realities of this place: the lack of education, the poor infrastructure (the town is dependent on power looms but the electricity goes for eight to ten hours at a time), the fragile peace between Hindus and Muslims, the lack of opportunity. There is a heartbreaking scene in which Akram talks about how he desperately wants to move to Mumbai and work in Bollywood, but has never been able to bridge the miles between his town and the big city. His ambition—he studies foreign films, reads and writes poetry—seems destined to be snuffed out.

But the documentary turns these men into stars. Shafique was so pleased with his acting career that at the end of the film, he expressed a desire to someday do a role like one of Amitabh Bachchan's. That never came to pass. Shafique died three years later, of mouth cancer. He was twenty-five. However, *Supermen of Malegaon* put him in the spotlight—the film travelled to several festivals, including the Indian Film Festival of Los Angeles.

These men and their good-natured struggle are reminders that showbiz might be a brutal business, but if you have the ardour, you will find a way to tell your story, and if you're lucky, you will find an audience for it.

You can watch *Supermen of Malegaon* on YouTube.

33

Kabhi Khushi Kabhie Gham . . .

Our earliest movie experiences are all about pleasure. Before the appreciation of storytelling, composition, technique or subtext kicks in, there is the basic, visceral response of joy. That's why it's called entertainment. One of the films that's given me countless hours of joy is Karan Johar's *Kabhi Khushi Kabhie Gham* . . .

Released in 2001, *K3G* was the grand finale of Bollywood's family drama trend, which started with Sooraj Barjatya's *Hum Aapke Hain Koun . . !* in 1994 and was cemented by Aditya Chopra's *Dilwale Dulhania Le Jayenge* in 1995. After all, there was little chance that any filmmaker could top the high-pitched melodrama, the dazzling array of stars, the staggering opulence and the unapologetic consumer porn (the weepy family reunion takes place in a London shopping mall) of this film. Post-*K3G*, Hindi cinema could only go 'desi' (*Lagaan*, released earlier that year, had already laid the foundation for the shift in sensibility).

I don't remember why or where, but Karan had narrated the story of *K3G* to me before he started making the film. The image that stayed with me from his narration was of the estranged brothers, Rohan and Rahul, sitting on a bench in London (years later in an interview, I asked him why so many of his films feature benches. He said that it had once come up in a conversation with his therapist, who explained that it might have something to do with a red bench from his school days, on which he usually sat alone, enjoying his isolation). I didn't understand then how the gluttonous, overweight Ladoo could grow up to be Hrithik Roshan, but I couldn't wait to see him and Shah Rukh Khan together on that bench. That frame just felt like magic.

Both *Lagaan* and *Dil Chahta Hai* released the same year. Compared to those films, *K3G* seemed creatively tame— essentially the same wine in a more extravagant bottle. In my review for *India Today* magazine, I described the film as 'Bollywood's first designer film' and 'sumptuous eye candy'. I wasn't wholly seduced by it. I found the emotions of the second half 'synthetic' and wrote that Rohan and Poo were 'underwritten characters'.

In the years since, I've come to love it more. I can't pinpoint how it happened but, over time, watching *K3G* became a ritual for the extended Chopra clan—a dozen of us get together at least once a year for a vacation and inevitably, on one evening, we sit and revisit the Raichand saga. We marvel, yet again, at the finery of the costumes by Manish Malhotra (Yashvardhan Raichand's Jamevar shawls are stunning, as is Poo's unending wardrobe) and the glitter and beauty of the songs by Farah Khan ('*Suraj Hua Maddham*' and '*Bole Chudiyan*' are my favourites). We swoon over Shah Rukh's entry—arguably his finest—as he gets out of a private plane into the helicopter and then walks in slo-mo from the helicopter toward the mansion, where his mother intuitively senses he is coming and waits by the door. The emotions are dialled up and someone, sometimes, gets teary. But we also laugh at scenes that come off as silly and synthetic. '*Keh diya na, bas keh diya*' is a favourite dialogue. So is Poo's legendary line: 'Tell me how it was'. In fact, Poo is the family favourite. Of all the characters in the film, the ditzy, clueless fashionista is the most enduring and endearing—her vanity and superficiality combined with, as she would say, 'good looks, good looks, good looks', are irresistible.

There is little doubt that *K3G* is overblown and overwrought, but it continues to exert a grip because Karan skilfully combined the gloss with drama that is, despite the heightened pitch, heartfelt. All the leads in the film weep copiously (usually with the title song blaring in the background). And Karan unabashedly manipulates the viewer, adding to the familial entanglements a generous dose of Hindu '*sanskars*' (Karva Chauth, *aartis*) and a dollop of patriotism (the Rohan-arriving-in-London montage is set to an upbeat '*Vande Mataram*', almost as if the film wants to remind us that despite his cool-kid flash, Rohan is an old-school Indian, who has come all this way to find his older brother). Nothing in this story or its telling (a mansion in Buckinghamshire substituted for the Raichand home in Delhi; the family's monogrammed helicopter; the licence plates on the family Rolls Royce, which read YR 1) is realistic, but the emotions land. Which is why the film continues to be both watchable and fodder for memes and blogs.

There's also that exquisitely romantic scene between Rahul and Anjali set at a Chandni Chowk mela—he's pushing green bangles down her wrist as he talks about '*dil ke rishtey*' and asking if it pricks. When he finally gets them down, he asks one more time and she nods. He says '*Mujhe bhi.*' That specific scene has more than seven million views on YouTube. That chemistry doesn't get old.

You can watch *K3G* on Amazon Prime.

34

Kalyug

Two warring families. Twisted secrets. A deadly business rivalry that can end only in tragedy. This is how director Shyam Benegal and producer Shashi Kapoor reimagined the Mahabharata in modern India.

In *Kalyug* (1981), the Pandavas and the Kauravas become the Puranchand and the Khubchand dynasties. The film is set during the Licence Raj and the battle is focused on government contracts, trade unions, profits and power. Like the Pandavas and the Kauravas, the Puranchands and the Khubchands are related. They maintain an outward demeanour of civility while playing a lethal game of one-upmanship behind the scenes.

Rekha, beauteous, simmering with an anger that she cannot express, plays the Draupadi figure. Supriya is married to the eldest Puranchand son, Dharam Raj, but her affections clearly lie with his brother, the volatile Bharat, played by Anant Nag. In contrast to her detached, passive husband, Bharat is a decisive man of action. But the aggression that fuels him also clouds his judgement and pushes him to decisions that destroy both families.

A.K. Hangal is Bhisham Chand or Dadaji, the Bhishma figure who tries in vain to make peace between the cousins. Dadaji works with the Khubchand family. On the other side, the elderly voice of wisdom is provided by Savitri, the Kunti figure, played with empathy by Sushma Seth. Savitri is a matriarch who suffers for the greater good of the *khandaan*. A superbly seething Victor Banerjee is Dhan Raj, the Duryodhana equivalent, a man blinded by rage and a thirst for revenge. And then there is Shashi Kapoor, heartbreakingly handsome, as Karan, Savitri's eldest son, born out of wedlock, and a good man on the wrong side.

Benegal and his writers—Girish Karnad co-wrote the screenplay and Satyadev Dubey, the dialogue—aren't interested in simplistic heroes and villains. What gives *Kalyug* its enduring power is the complexity of the narrative. All the characters are flawed; most are propelled by a mix of hubris and greed. Savitri and Bhisham Chand try to steer the course of events but any compromise in this corporate battle is seen as weakness. And once Bhisham Chand is edged out of the Khubchand company, all rules of propriety go with him. Gross manipulation, bribery, even murder become acceptable business practices.

Kalyug is one of the first films I saw that showcased the lifestyles of the very rich. The action unravels in sprawling homes and plush apartments; there is horse-racing, nightclubs, golf courses, uniformed staff, Western classical music and foreign cars. But unlike in the films of Yash Chopra, this world is presented (by cinematographer Govind Nihalani) without a glossy sheen. So even as we admire the art on the walls and the beautiful clothes (Rekha's silk kurtas and saris are especially striking; the costumes were by Jennifer Kendal), we understand the price they've paid for these trappings. Their wealth is not a comfortable cushion that makes their trials easier to bear; it is the reason these characters have lost their moorings. *Kalyug* plays out like a grim morality tale.

Benegal tells the story with minimal fuss and melodrama. In one of the finest scenes, Savitri goes to Karan's house and reveals to him that he is also her son. She wants to avert more bloodshed. It's an emotionally devastating moment, which has even more power because it is staged without shrillness. Karan staggers backwards (I've never forgotten the traumatized look in Kapoor's eyes) and the scene cuts to him curled up in bed in a foetal position. His world, everything he thought he knew, has come undone. His large sea-facing apartment seems now to mock the hollowness of his life.

This undertow of sadness pervades *Kalyug*. Vanraj Bhatia's haunting score sets the tone right in the opening credits— we see visuals of a busy factory teeming with men and heavy machinery, but it isn't framed as a scene of modernity or progress. Bhatia's ominous notes forewarn us that there is trouble ahead. The same music plays as the end titles roll against the looming buildings of Bombay, almost as though Benegal were indicting the city itself, a city that runs on commerce and competition.

Each time I watch *Kalyug*, I find myself admiring afresh Kapoor's courage and cinematic taste. At the time, he was at the peak of his career, doing hearty masala movies like *Shaan* and *Do Aur Do Paanch*. But his aesthetic sensibility, rooted in theatre, was more refined.

In 1978, three years before *Kalyug*, Kapoor and Benegal collaborated on the brilliant period saga *Junoon*. In it, Kapoor plays Javed Khan, a Pathan who becomes obsessed with a young British girl. It's an intricate role without a happy ending, but it was still more in the mould of a leading man. In *Kalyug*, Kapoor is a key player but he is part of an ensemble cast—the film is a veritable directory of theatre and art-house names, including Vijaya Mehta, Om Puri and Amrish Puri. Kapoor was the biggest name and the producer of *Kalyug*, and yet the film doesn't project him as a hero or burnish his stardom. Like everyone else, he simply serves the narrative.

Which is one more reason to seek out the film. You can find substandard copies online, but a DVD is likely to offer the richest experience.

35

C/o Kancharapalem

Some movies work like minor miracles. They arrive with no fanfare or publicity. They have minuscule budgets and feature unknown actors, so they aren't instantly seductive. These films work purely on the strength of their artistry. And they prove that, ultimately, story and talent are the real stars. The 2018 Telugu film *C/o Kancharapalem* is one such work.

Kancharapalem is a small town near Visakhapatnam. The film is about four romances set here: between schoolchildren Sunitha and Sundaram; between Bhargavi and Joseph, who are in their early twenties; between Gaddam and Saleema, who are in their thirties; and between Raju, a forty-nine-year-old bachelor, and his forty-two-year-old boss, a government officer whom he addresses as 'Madam'.

Raju is the central figure. The film opens with him beginning his day, his banter with the neighbours, his exercise routine, his prayers; him making his way through the narrow lanes of Kancharapalem (the film was shot entirely on location in that town) to his office. Raju is an amiable, hard-working man who is at peace with his place in the world, but the fact that he is single presents a vexing problem for the people of Kancharapalem, who take a keen interest in each other's lives. At one point, they even hold a town-hall-style meeting to discuss why Raju never married and what his sexual orientation might be. Raju maintains that things just didn't work out for him, and the meeting dissolves, the community at a loss and unable to help.

Raju's story is intercut with the three other love stories. Characters from one story don't enter the other and we only discover at the end how the various threads interconnect. Director Venkatesh Maha, who has also written the story and screenplay, exerts precise control over the world he has created, doling out exactly the information we need to stay invested in the characters and their tangled lives. Each story reaches its own crisis and conclusion.

Within these romances, Venkatesh slips in musings about gender, religion, dignity of labour, and how toxic men—controlling, emotionally and physically abusive fathers and brothers—circumscribe and wreck the lives of women, even those they claim to love. But the storytelling doesn't dramatically underline this. Venkatesh isn't interested in heroes and villains. He is presenting life, unfurling in all its messy splendour. There is compassion in his gaze. And critically, he locates the humour in the seemingly humdrum routines of this sleepy town—so in one story, eloping becomes a challenge because the woman can't run fast enough. She has to sit down and catch her breath. These small observations make the film.

C/o Kancharapalem is also a masterclass in how to write female characters. The women in the film are astounding. One of the stories features a sex worker who refuses to be apologetic about who she is and what she does. When a man proposes marriage, she rebuffs him saying, don't think you're a hero for rescuing me from a life that I have chosen.

When he persists, she eventually agrees, with a few conditions—until they marry, she will continue to work and he will drop her to her corner every day; he will also tell his friends who sought out her services that he's in love with her; and he will take her to a movie and a meal at a fancy restaurant. The man agrees, gets down on his knees, gifts her a bottle of Mansion House, her preferred brand of alcohol, and declares that he loves her. It's a grand romantic gesture between two people who live threadbare lives but have the same longing for human connection.

There's also Radha, the government officer who insists that Raju, a clerk, sit with her and the other officers for lunch. She's a widow with a twenty-year-old daughter; she and Raju get along well. She takes the lead and proposes marriage. And when her brother opposes the match, Madam's feisty daughter asks him at what age women can make decisions about their own lives.

None of the messaging is heavy-handed. The film, instead, has a quiet lyricism. Even heartbreak, and there's plenty of it, is portrayed with tenderness. The cast is made up largely of non-professionals who were picked from Kancharapalem. In some scenes, you can see the rawness, but it's not jarring. Instead, there is something gentle and unforced about these actors, who include Praveena Paruchuri (one of the producers of the film) as Saleema. Subba Rao Vepada as Raju holds the multiple strands of the narrative together.

C/o Kancharapalem radiates with humanity and a lightness of being. It is of course a love story, but it's also so much more. There is a generosity of heart in the storytelling that shines through in its unvarnished visuals.

You can watch the film on Netflix and on YouTube.

36

Loins of Punjab Presents

A belligerent, political, bursting-with-attitude Bhangra rapper who calls himself Turbanotorious BDG is in an elevator holding hands with his male lover. On one floor, the door opens to reveal a snooty society maven and her servile singing guru. She is holding her precious dog in her hands. The lady, guru and dog take in the sight and pause, a fraction too long, on the hands. To which BDG responds with, 'What you looking at, bitch?' And debutant director Manish Acharya cuts to a close-up of the dog.

It's a tiny, not-particularly-pivotal moment in the film, but it captures the essence of *Loins of Punjab Presents* (2007)— scrappy, funny and blessedly hell-bent on inclusion. The set-up is simple: over the course of a weekend, several contestants gather in a New Jersey hotel to compete in Desi Idol, an American Idol-style singing competition. The prize money is $25,000. The competition is sponsored by an Indian-owned company that specializes in pork loins. The founder, J.K. Singhal, came to the United States with nothing, but built an empire on loins, and we're told 'in the biz, he was known as loin king', which Hindi film lovers will instantly recognize as a reference to one of the great movie villains, Ajit Khan. Ajit's signature dialogue (delivered in the 1976 film *Kalicharan*) was, '*Saara shehar mujhe lion ke naam se jaanta hai*,' except lion was pronounced loin.

The Desi Idol contestants include the self-anointed queen of Long Island, Rrita Kapoor (played by a deliciously Machiavellian Shabana Azmi); Preeti Patel, hands down the best singer, who is accompanied by her gregarious Gujarati family, headed by Darshan Jariwala as Sanjeev Patel (in one of the film's funniest scenes, Sanjeev tries to bribe an obviously gay judge by taking him to a strip joint and then asks, 'You want Coke?' pronouncing Coke like cock); Turbanotorious BDG who, underneath all the tough talk, is an insecure artist who needs his boyfriend to pep him up; and Josh Cohen (Michael Raimondi), the sole white contestant, who is a lover of all things Indian. He's at the competition with his Indian girlfriend Opama, played by Ayesha Dharker. The others routinely mistake him for a waiter.

The film is constructed as a mockumentary, with freeze-frames, asides and characters addressing the camera. The shoestring budget is apparent in the drab visuals and dependence on close-ups. Almost the entire film takes place indoors. But Manish and co-writer Anuvab Pal (who also plays one of the contestants) make up for all this with their sparkling storytelling. *Loins of Punjab Presents* is determined to entertain, but Manish and Anuvab also layer in insightful commentary, especially about Bollywood and the vice-like grip it retains on Indians worldwide.

The film both celebrates and pokes fun at the Hindi film industry. So a news reporter asks if Bollywood is culturally bankrupt, but we also get a contestant from New York who can't speak Hindi but dreams of moving to Mumbai and becoming an actor in Bollywood because it's 'pre-cynical'. The laughs come with an emotional undercurrent that gathers momentum, culminating in a rousing climax that might make your eyes well up. Hint: the national anthem features.

It raises interesting questions, such as: Who qualifies as a custodian of Indian culture? At one point in the film, the desi contestants rebel against the inclusion of Josh—some carry signs that read 'Desi rules' and 'Go home foreigners'. But, the film asks, who is a foreigner and what is home?

Jameel Khan plays Mr Bokade, the head of the event management company that organizes Desi Idol. This is a man who lunges on and off hotel beds to check the springs, just in case he should find a willing partner. Bokade is a greasy hustler but he delivers the film's key message—when the contest is over, a reporter says, 'But you must find it strange that a desi did not win, that an outsider won.' Bokade replies with exasperation, '*Arre* what outsider, who is outsider? We are outsider no, in America, but we are insider. We are outsider inside and now that we are inside, can we keep people outside, especially when they are already inside? So forget all this outside, inside. We are all inside even if we were outside once. Understood?'

Bokade's declaration resonates sharply in an increasingly splintered world. *Loins of Punjab Presents* is set after the 9/11 attacks. Manish and Anuvab are keenly aware of the consequences of being a person of colour in America at this point in history, but they choose to address it with humour—so an elderly, white couple who are guests at the Desi Idol competition are convinced that at least a few of the Indians are planning to plant a bomb. Everyone is wary of anyone whose skin tone is different from their own. But ultimately, music and Bollywood conquer all.

Loins of Punjab Presents didn't fit into any existing mould: it was a film in English, about Non-Resident Indians, hinting at serious things but brimming with good cheer and filmi music. And yet it ran for seven weeks in Mumbai and travelled to a slew of film festivals, picking up audience awards.

Tragically, the film was also Manish's last feature: he died in an accident in December 2010. But his warm presence radiates through the film, both off-screen and on. Manish played the contestant Vikram Tejwani, a number-crunching financial analyst who loves Hindi cinema and whose job has been outsourced to India. He doesn't win the competition but he meets the love of his life through it.

Loins of Punjab Presents insists that the world might be flawed and fumbling, but eventually we will all come out winners if our hearts are in the right place. It's a distinctly Bollywood message, and a chance to put the rose-tinted spectacles back on, at least for a while.

You can watch the film on YouTube or on iTunes.

37

Masoom

There are some faces designed for a movie close-up. Think of Madhubala, tantalizingly sexy yet artless, singing '*Aaiye Meharbaan*' in *Howrah Bridge* (1958); or Hrithik Roshan, with granite body and greying hair, making that slow-motion entry in *War* (2019); or Aishwarya Rai, impossibly beautiful, keeping the *diya* burning in '*Silsila Ye Chaahat Ka*' in *Devdas* (2002); or Jugal Hansraj, cherubic, with pensive, pained hazel-green eyes, in *Masoom* (1983).

Jugal was only nine when he made his feature-film debut as Rahul, the son born outside marriage, desperately seeking his missing father. Director Shekhar Kapur, who had never made a film until then, or even assisted on one, instinctively understood that Jugal was his secret weapon. He was *Masoom*, the very personification of innocence. His disarming sweetness made it impossible for viewers to judge his parents or, eventually, hold their own emotions in check. Even without dialogue, his face could wring tears from your heart.

Which is why we don't fully see it until about 45 minutes into the film. Rahul makes his entry even before the opening credits: we hear his breathing, rushed and frazzled, as he runs to be by his dying mother's side. The titles roll against an image of him as a silhouette, standing by her funeral pyre. In another scene, we see his profile. These glimpses give us a sense of his abject loneliness. And then finally, when he is sitting in a car with his father—who he doesn't yet know is his father—we get a frontal close-up, accompanied by a question that his father cannot answer: '*Aap meri* mummy *ko jaante the?*'

Masoom is an uncredited adaptation of Erich Segal's novel *Man, Woman and Child*, about a married man who discovers that he has a son with another woman. Shekhar and Gulzar Saab, who wrote the screenplay, dialogue and lyrics, transplanted the story to an affluent family in Delhi. D.K. and Indu are happily married. He is a successful architect. She is a proud homemaker who dresses impeccably and notices when even a single vase is out of place. They have two adorable daughters, Pinky and Minni. It's a picture-perfect home, but early in the film, a pet dog jumps onto a side-table and causes a framed family photo to fall and shatter, foreshadowing what is to come.

D.K. discovers that a casual liaison, on a school reunion trip, produced a son. The woman is now dead and he is in charge of a boy he has never met. D.K. and Indu's decade-long marriage comes apart. This fraying is portrayed with precision and delicacy. D.K. tells Indu about his infidelity as she is taking pillows out of a cupboard to make their bed. It's a routine domestic ritual, now heavy with humiliation, regret and resentment. Their home is their sanctuary. D.K. has shattered its peace. But he isn't a villain. He's a loving husband and doting father who once made a terrible decision. In one of the film's finest scenes, Indu tears into D.K. And D.K., exhausted and broken, replies, '*Toh kya karoon, sooli chadh jaoon?*'

Shekhar and Gulzar Saab create flesh-and-blood characters who are flawed and struggling. Indu cannot bring herself to forgive D.K. or accept Rahul. She understands that he is blameless, but his very being is a reminder of D.K.'s betrayal and she cannot tolerate that. Underneath her tasteful saris (designed by film journalist Bhawana Somaaya), she is a raw wound. When, one day, Rahul cuts himself, rushes to her and instinctively shouts, 'Mummy,' she snaps at him, '*Main tumhari mummy nahin hoon.*'

This could have come off as unnecessarily cruel, but Shabana Azmi imbues Indu's scars with dignity. Even at her most broken, this woman has strength and the ability to hold this fractured family together. It's a formidable portrayal because Shabana doesn't try to heighten the drama. Neither does Naseeruddin Shah, who is equally attuned to D.K.'s anguish. D.K.'s lapse is appalling. We can't defend his actions. But because Naseer plays him with such honest conviction, we sympathize with his suffering. We hope that somehow this family will find a way through.

Incredibly (for 1983 at least), the children are written and enacted like real children. Rahul, Pinky (Urmila Matondkar, making her feature-film debut) and Minni (played with industrial-strength cuteness by Aradhana Srivastav) are fearful of the emotional shifts in the adult world. They demand time and attention and can be annoying. But because they are unaware and non-judgemental, they are also wonderfully accommodating. So the younger daughter Minni automatically starts to call Rahul '*bhaiya*', to which Indu responds, '*Yeh bhaiya kab se ho gaya?*'

The film also benefits enormously from R.D. Burman's poignant soundtrack. In a 2011 interview with the *Indian Express*, Gulzar Saab recalled that when he started to write the screenplay, the lines '*Tujhse Naaraz Nahin Zindagi*' came to mind and became the emotional foundation of the film. 'After that,' he said, 'I just followed the characters and let the words navigate them for me.' While the title song provided adults with a perspective on life, '*Lakdi ki Kathi*' became the anthem for a generation of children. Burman and Gulzar Saab created a song that was inventive and inspired. '*Lakdi ki Kathi*' is, in the best sense of the word, childlike.

Parts of *Masoom* haven't aged well. There is a clumsy subplot involving Indu's friend Chanda, played by Tanuja, who is positioned as an 'independent woman'. This is conveyed to us through the facts that Chanda smokes and runs a successful business. Chanda is estranged from her husband. She proudly declares that she needs no one, but then promptly returns to her family because her son asks her to. She makes a half-baked reference to maternal love, which is perhaps meant to explain why Indu finally accepts Rahul.

There are also a few problematic lines in the film about the importance of a son. Early on, D.K. playfully ribs Indu about not having one. D.K.'s closest friend Suri (a sparkling Saeed Jaffrey) talks about the pleasures of watching one's son become a man. When D.K. and Rahul are together, they do the things we never see D.K. do with his daughters: camping, horseback-riding. In these moments, *Masoom* seems to suggest that a family is incomplete without a boy. It's oddly archaic for a film otherwise so far ahead of its time.

But the decades haven't dimmed the power of the drama and emotions in *Masoom*. It continues to be a three-hankie weeper.

You can watch the film on Amazon Prime.

38

Mirch Masala

In Ketan Mehta's *Mirch Masala*, men sometimes refer to women as spicy. The connotation is sexual. The men are deeming the women desirable. But, as they find out, '*mirch*' can also be deadly.

Based on a short story by Chunilal Madia, *Mirch Masala* (1987) is set in the Rann of Kutch in the 1940s. The dull, brown landscape of the parched riverside village is broken by swathes of flaming red chillies spread on the ground, and by the women, who wear red mirrored *ghaghras* and bright *odhnis*. They mirror the chillies that they grind all day in a masala factory. Like the chillies, they are fire. And there is much that they must burn.

Mirch Masala is a story of systemic oppression. The women in the village function with minimal freedom. They are subservient to the men, who abuse them emotionally and physically: husbands beat wives, fathers beat daughters. Throughout the film, we see women toiling—fetching water, feeding animals, working in the factory, giving birth—while the men loiter or gossip. The most powerful man in the village is the *mukhi* (Suresh Oberoi), who slaps his wife in public, manhandles his young daughter, and insists that he must keep a mistress because it is expected of a man in his position.

The village is plagued by illiteracy, ignorance, caste, class. The rumblings of dissent unfolding in the rest of the country haven't penetrated yet: in one scene, a character asks '*Swaraj hoti kya cheez hai?*' All of which makes it easy for the *subedar*, an officer of the British government, to treat the village like his personal fiefdom. This character, played with perfect imperiousness and manic aggression by Naseeruddin Shah, is cruel and despotic. His masculinity seems to reside in his moustache, which he twirls with pride. The villagers serve him like subjects serving their monarch. They scramble to meet his demands, whether it's paying taxes or fawning over his obsession, a gramophone, or providing him with women for pleasure.

One person refuses to fall in line: Sonbai, played by a stunning, smouldering Smita Patil. When the *subedar* first rides into the village along with his soldiers, Sonbai is the only woman who doesn't see them and run. She stands her ground and meets his eye. He is intrigued. After her husband leaves to work in the town, the *subedar* demands that Sonbai come to him. Like the phonograph, she becomes an obsession.

When he pushes too far, Sonbai slaps him. A brilliantly mounted chase sequence follows as the *subedar*'s men, on horseback, try to capture her. Rajat Dholakia's thumping music and Jehangir Choudhary's camera capture the furious action as Sonbai, hair and *ghaghra* askew, flees. At one point, she hides behind large mounds of chillies that are being dried in the sun. She seems to become one with the spice. Eventually, she runs into the factory, where the women work, and shuts herself in.

Sonbai's defiant stand snowballs into a fight that puts everyone at risk—the *subedar* threatens to let his men pillage and destroy the village unless she relents. The men of the village are willing to trade Sonbai for peace. From the *mukhi* to the pandit, they all try and convince her to make this 'sacrifice'. But the village teacher, who is a Gandhian, fights for her. As does Abu Miya, the elderly factory guard (Om Puri, unforgettable in his righteous rage). Abu Miya is the sole Muslim character in the film. In the end, he does his namaz and picks up his gun. His stand is clear: '*Zulm ki marzi nahin chalegi.*'

The battle between Sonbai and the *subedar* culminates in one of Hindi cinema's most striking climaxes—chillies play a prominent role.

Mirch Masala is a potent celebration of female strength (many of the male characters don't even have names). The last shot is a close-up of Sonbai's face, bathed in red. She's holding a sickle and looks like an avenging goddess. Sonbai propels the story, but the screenplay (by Ketan Mehta, Shafi Hakim, Hriday Lani and Tripurari Sharma) also allows ample room for other female characters to assert themselves. There's Saraswati (Deepti Naval), the *mukhi's* wife, who pushes against the patriarchy before Sonbai does. Saraswati demands accountability from her philandering husband and insists on putting their daughter in school. There's Radha (Supriya Pathak), who dares to romance the *mukhi's* brother. There's Lakhvi (Ratna Pathak Shah), who, in the most matter-of-fact way, sleeps with the *subedar* for money.

The women don't all side with Sonbai instantly. The elderly Maanki (Dina Pathak) sagely advises her to acquiesce because '*izzat ameeron ka shauk hai*'. Another tells Sonbai that the fault is in her looks. To which Sonbai retorts with anger, '*Uske dekhne mein nahin?*' The age-old argument that a woman asked for it is decimated in a single line.

Throughout the film, these women are photographed behind beautiful, latticed grilles, perhaps to suggest imprisonment.

Our last view of Saraswati is her banging against the window of her home, where her husband has bolted her in. But the spirit of defiance cannot be contained. The other women, if only briefly, have emerged victorious. You can sense a change brewing.

Mirch Masala is a visually sumptuous, rousing feminist anthem. You can watch it on Mubi India.

39

Sairat

Just as the hero of a film is only as good as its villain, a love story is only as good as its opposition. The intensity of emotion is directly proportional to the conflict. The wider the gap that the lovers must bridge, the deeper the ache.

In *Mughal-e-Azam* (1960), the hurdle is status: the heir to the Mughal empire falls in love with a dancing girl. In *Qayamat Se Qayamat Tak* (1988) and *Goliyon Ki Raasleela Ram-Leela* (2013), both adaptations of Romeo and Juliet, it's warring families. In *Dilwale Dulhania Le Jayenge* (1995), it is definitions of 'Hindustani'—Simran's father wants her to marry a man from Punjab because he believes that Kuljeet is more authentically Indian. Of course, Raj, born and raised in the UK, eventually proves him wrong. Being properly Indian is not a function of geography, the movie tells us, it's a function of your moral compass.

In *Bombay* (1995), the conflict is religion—Shekhar comes from an orthodox Hindu family and Shaila Bano is Muslim.

Sairat (2016), which belongs in the pantheon of great love stories, tackles a villain that mainstream Indian cinema has largely steered clear of: caste.

The Constitution of India deemed the caste system illegal, but its oppressive stratification continues to be a horrific lived reality for millions. Which is why *Sairat* (Marathi for Wild), must necessarily end in tragedy. Sixty-nine years after Independence, for a lower-caste boy and an upper-caste girl, there can still be no happy ending.

The film starts in Bitter Gaon, a village in Maharashtra. Parshya's father is a fisherman. Archie's father is an affluent landlord and a heavyweight politician. Both youngsters are in their first year of college. He is besotted with her. She slowly starts to reciprocate his feelings. For the first hour, as Archie and Parshya fall headlong into love, *Sairat* plays out like a swoony fantasy, but without the synthetic textures that you might find in a Bollywood romance. *Sairat* was shot on location and the visuals are realistic. The settings, clothes and faces aren't glossy. These are regular people, who pause to dance in the swaying green fields because love has transported them.

This is the genius of *Sairat*. Writer-director Nagraj Manjule uses the vocabulary of the Bollywood love story to craft a searing critique of the caste system and a film that lands like a body blow. To begin with, Nagraj cast non-professional newbies Akash Thosar and Rinku Rajguru as Parshya and Archie. Akash was a wrestler and Rinku was a class nine student. According to media reports, Akash was spotted at the railway station in Solapur and asked to audition for the role.

Unlike groomed-to-the-gills Bollywood debutants, Akash and Rinku don't come off as constructed. Both are natural-born actors who carry the weight of the film without faltering once. The ordinariness of their manner makes Archie and Parshya instantly relatable. What's larger-than-life is their heady passion. Their exhilarating love story is further buoyed by Ajay-Atul's sumptuous soundtrack. Nagraj uses the music like an orchestra conductor to immerse us in their feelings. The rousing song 'Yad Lagla', which roughly translates to 'I've gone insane', captures—in slow motion—the rising tide of emotion between the two. He leaps off a boat when he hears her name. She smiles a little when he passes, too close to her, at the village well. Even if you don't understand a word of Marathi (I don't), the joyous symphony conveys flawlessly what these two are experiencing.

Archie is the firecracker in the relationship. Her privileged upbringing gives her a confidence that Parshya simply doesn't have. In one scene, in the classroom, she simply turns and stares at him for so long that he gets embarrassed and leaves. She rides horses and drives a tractor and a Bullet motorcycle. She tells Parshya's friends, Langdya and Sallya, not to chew tobacco. She also insists they call Langdya by his real name, Pradeep; he shouldn't be defined by his limp. Archie is more refined than they are. She's also bossy, but her entitlement is combined with generosity. Which is not the case with her brother, named, without irony, Prince.

The film opens with a local cricket match (amusingly called the Bitter Gaon Premier League, in which Parshya is captaining the village team. When Prince walks on stage as an honoured guest, he is introduced as a youth leader and 'the future of Maharashtra'. Prince embodies a toxic mix of patriarchy, upper-class and upper-caste entitlement. It's telling that Nagraj, a Dalit filmmaker, doing a cameo as the commentator, makes the announcement. He's setting the ground for the horrors to follow because he, more than most others, understands the ways in which men like Prince still rule the world.

Nagraj's script inserts these disturbing signs throughout the film. At the same cricket match, Archie's father, the powerful

Patil Tatya, dismisses his political rivals by asking how they will control the affairs of the district when they can't even control their women. These words will come to haunt Tatya when his daughter also escapes the shackles put on her. This is a man who loves his daughter—their house is named Archana after her—but she cannot break the ironclad rules of caste and clan without horrific consequences.

In another scene, in a college classroom, Prince slaps a professor who is reprimanding him for talking on the phone during a lecture. The professor is teaching them about the Dalit poet Namdeo Dhasal, co-founder of the Dalit Panthers. It's a critical detail that, once again, reminds us what the stakes are in this love story.

Post-interval, the film shifts gears. Like hundreds of lovers in Indian cinema, Archie and Parshya run away. But once again, Nagraj subverts the formula. He doesn't romanticize the experience. Unlike the lovers in *Qayamat Se Qayamat Tak* or *Love Story* (1981), Archie and Parshya don't start living a fairy-tale life in a quaint little cottage. They end up in a slum in Hyderabad. She retches when she has to use the common bathroom. Parshya has to spend some of their meagre money to buy her bottled water because she can't bring herself to drink what he can. Reality hits hard. Archie weeps with longing for her family and her comfortable home. And their relationship is put to such an extreme test that it almost splinters.

Sairat runs for nearly three hours. Before watching the film, I wondered why any contemporary filmmaker would opt for such a punishing runtime. After watching it, I understood why the narrative is so expansive. Because Nagraj wants us to invest wholly in Archie and Parshya's journey. We must experience the evolution of their relationship—from giddy teenage ardour to a more mature understanding of each other. We must become their allies so that when their brutal end arrives, it fells not just Archie and Parshya, but also us.

I watched *Sairat* in a theatre, almost four weeks after it came out. It had already become the most successful Marathi film in history. I sat in a single-screen cinema that, even on a weekday, was reasonably packed. The experience was heady—when the song '*Zingaat*' began, people got up and started dancing. There was a collective euphoria. But that sense of joy leaked out soon after. When the film was over, we walked out in silence. There was none of the usual chatter. I felt like I had been gutted.

Underneath the romance and music, *Sairat* simmers with a rage that will scar you. Which is why you must watch it.

Sairat is streaming on Zee5 and on YouTube.

40

The Namesake

What constitutes home? In her elegiac and eloquent 2006 film *The Namesake*, Mira Nair grapples with this thorny question. An adaptation of Jhumpa Lahiri's novel of the same name, *The Namesake* follows the lives of two generations of a Bengali family. Ashoke Ganguli, an engineer, and Ashima, an aspiring classical singer, have an arranged marriage and move from Calcutta (Kolkata) to New York City in the late 1970s.

The story spans several decades as Ashoke and Ashima, two strangers, slowly fall in love, have children, and the family, now a mix of first- and second-generation immigrants, negotiates the tightrope between tradition and modernity, between holding on and letting go, between what is properly Indian, and more importantly Bengali, and what is American.

The West has routinely been part of Hindi cinema, but usually as an attractive, aspirational backdrop for songs. Foreign locations came into fashion in the 1960s, with Raj Kapoor's *Sangam* (1964), in which the lead characters went on an extended European honeymoon, and Shakti Samanta's *An Evening in Paris* (1967), a thriller set in the French capital.

One of the earliest films to focus on the lives of Non-Resident Indians (NRIs) was Manoj Kumar's *Purab aur Paschim* in 1970. In that film, the West (represented by London) is depicted as seductive but spiritually fatal: there is an assortment of unsavoury characters who, living far away from the motherland, have lost their moral moorings. The NRI children smoke, drink and go to nightclubs. Of course, they are duly reformed by the hero, who is named Bharat (in case you missed the point).

This cliché of the debauched, culturally lost Indian immigrant was turned on its head by *Dilwale Dulhania Le Jayenge*. Raj and Simran, both born and brought up in London, clad in stylish leather jackets, her in miniskirts, are unfailingly moral—so much so that they can spend a night together in a hotel without having sex because Raj understands, as he puts it, what honour means for a Hindustani woman. *DDLJ* successfully sold the fantasy of the global desi: someone who is at once trendy and traditional.

The Namesake isn't interested in these simplistic oppositions or undemanding hybrids. Working from a screenplay by Sooni Taraporevala, Mira creates a compassionate and deeply moving portrait of the longing for roots. At the centre of this fractured cultural identity is the name of Ashoke and Ashima's son—Gogol, which comes from Nikolai Gogol, Ashoke's favourite Russian writer. The author's most famous work, *The Overcoat*, plays a significant role in Ashoke's life. He is reading it while on a train from Calcutta to Jamshedpur, which crashes. He is still holding on to the book when he is rescued, bleeding and broken, from the debris.

Ashoke miraculously survives and Gogol becomes his connection with his country and an emblem of good luck. In a deeply moving scene, Ashoke explains the reason for his unusual name to his son. He says, 'You remind me of every day that followed. Every day since then has been a gift.'

But Gogol is ambivalent about this pet name that his father impulsively gave him when he was born. As a toddler, he insists on it but as he grows up, he rejects it, preferring the more common Nikhil, which of course gets shortened to Nik. Nik is a New Yorker chasing his dream career with his American girlfriend by his side. He has little patience with Indian customs and is sometimes casually indifferent to his parents.

When his girlfriend asks him, 'Don't your parents want you to marry a nice Indian girl?' he says, 'I don't care what they want.' Which is not true. Because Nik is also Gogol, a sensitive young man who eventually comes to understand the journey and the sacrifice of his parents.

Kal Penn plumbs the dichotomy of Gogol, playing him with conviction both as the typical, rebellious, pot-smoking teenager and later as the mature, responsible adult. But *The Namesake* is held together by the richness of Irrfan Khan and Tabu's performances. Both give their characters a gentle dignity. Ashoke and Ashima are ordinary people who lead ordinary lives. There is no drama or plot twist. But a certain compassion and soulfulness suffuses every frame they are in.

One of my favourite scenes is at the airport—Ashoke is leaving Ashima's side for the first time in their long marriage, to take up a teaching job in Cleveland. He is standing in line to board the plane. She is a distance away, waving. He keeps looking at her, forgetting to move forward. The man behind him nudges him. And Ashoke says goodbye with a tilt of his head. The tenderness of the gesture tells you about the love they have built together. It's at once beautiful and heart-breaking.

Mira stages these scenes with absolute precision. *The Namesake* is a visually lush film, starting with the exquisite titles. Bengali lettering appears against rich reds and oranges as Nitin

Sawhney's haunting score plays in the background. The scene for a film that combines beauty with melancholy is instantly set. The music, a fusion of Bengali folk, hip-hop and classical sound, traverses time and cultures. Like the characters, it is at once specific and universal.

One of the most poignant moments in *The Namesake* is during a holiday that the family takes together. Gogol is a young boy. His sister is an infant. He and his father take a walk down a rocky pathway that juts into the ocean. When they get to the end, Ashoke realizes that he has left his camera in the car. He laughs and says, 'All this way, no picture. We just have to remember it then.' And Gogol asks, 'For how long do I have to remember it?'

It's an unforgettable exchange between father and son and it always brings tears to my eyes. As does Mira's end dedication: 'For our parents who gave us everything'.

Without being preachy or emotionally manipulative, *The Namesake* will make you reconsider your own relationships.

You can find the film on Disney+ Hotstar.

41

Udaan

'*Udna band karo, paon ko zameen pe rakho.*' These are instructions from a father to his son. But *Udaan*, a poignant, perceptive coming-of-age film, teaches us exactly the opposite. It reveals to us the importance of taking flight.

Udaan is the story of a seventeen-year-old boy named Rohan, who is expelled from his posh boarding school and forced to return home to live with his father, whom he hasn't seen for eight years. In that time, the man has remarried, had another son and gotten divorced. A six-year-old half-brother named Arjun now occupies Rohan's bedroom. And that's not the worst of it. Their father, Bhairav Singh, is an authoritarian, abusive, deeply frustrated alcoholic. He doesn't hesitate to use his fists when he lays down the law for his boys—for starters, they call him Sir. His anger, which is always at boiling point, singes their home. Happiness is impossible, but even calm seems out of reach.

Rohan is an artist. He writes poetry and creates fantastical stories that enthral listeners. But in his father's worldview, there is no room or respect for art. At one point, Bhairav dismissively tells his son, '*Ladka nahin, ladki ho tum.*' Bhairav insists that Rohan follow the more traditional Indian male path—he enrols the boy in an engineering college and puts him to work in his steel factory. Perhaps hoping that amid the heavy machinery and glowing furnaces, a man will be forged.

Udaan (2010) is a pointed examination of what constitutes masculinity. There are barely any women on screen. It's almost as if director Vikramaditya Motwane and his co-writer and co-producer Anurag Kashyap are demonstrating how men can become stunted in the absence of women. In a heart-breaking scene, Rohan and Arjun talk about their mothers. Rohan says he remembers how his mother smelled when he cuddled with her. Arjun has no memory of his. Later we see photographs of Rohan with his mother, who is smiling and holding him affectionately. Without her, their home is bereft of even basic human touch.

Bhairav is masculinity at its most toxic and limiting. His idea of strength is racing against his son and winning, controlling the lives of those who depend upon him, belittling their hopes and aspirations, drinking until he can no longer stand. Bhairav mocks Rohan's sensitivity and soft edges. He even mocks his brother Jimmy's inability to have a child. In his view, these traits exemplify failure. But Vikram and Anurag are too sophisticated as storytellers to give us a straight-up monster. Stray snatches of dialogue reveal the abuse Bhairav endured in his own childhood. His father was also an authoritarian man not averse to hitting his child. We see Bhairav's loneliness and how he suffers as a result of his inability to make real emotional connections—in one scene, he tells Rohan that he had come to meet him once, at his boarding school; he watched him from afar but didn't approach, he says, because he had nothing to say. There are other hints that underneath the bitter bully is a man who perhaps wishes he could be different; hints that perhaps Bhairav doesn't see his brother and his son as failures, but as contrasts that he can hardly bear.

Vikram tells the story with such precise control that it's hard to believe this was his first film. He skilfully builds up the dread so that we tense whenever Bhairav is around his boys—even if it is on a family picnic. We see a backshot of the four, Bhairav, Jimmy, Rohan and Arjun, sitting on benches. It's a snapshot of masculinity, each one suffering and struggling with his own demons. Even poor Arjun, whose tender age doesn't shield him.

The sparingly used background music underlines the harshness of their lives. DOP Mahendra J. Shetty doesn't add sheen to the visuals, but finds poetry in the industrial landscape of Jamshedpur, and in the faces of Aayan Boradia, who plays Arjun, and Rajat Barmecha, who plays Rohan.

Rajat has what Christopher Nolan describes as 'visual empathy'. You connect with him immediately. His face combines the tenderness of youth with kindness and intelligence. Early in the film, he recites one of his poems to a friend. It begins with '*Chhoti-chhoti chhitrayi yaaden, bichhi hui hain lamho ki* lawn *par / nange pair unpar chalte-chalte, itni door chale aaye / ki ab bhool gaye hain . . . ki joote kahan utaare the.*'

We barely know Rohan, but we believe that he could write this. Rohan gets up to the usual teenage mischief too: sneaking out of school to watch a movie, smoking, getting drunk. But there is something distinctive that sets him apart from the other boys his age. Rajat embodies his poet soul perfectly. Incidentally, the poetry, which is one of the highlights of the film, was written by Satyanshu Singh and Devanshu Singh, who went on to make their feature directorial debut with *Chintu Ka Birthday* in 2019.

Rohan resembles a sapling mid-bloom. In contrast, Bhairav is granite. Ronit Roy played him with such conviction that, for years, filmmakers continued to cast him in the role of imposing father. Ronit plumbed Bhairav's cruelty, but also his scars. By the end, you pity him. It's hard to imagine that the actor was originally cast in Jimmy's role. That role eventually went to Ram Kapoor, who brings a semblance of cheer and empathy to the film. Each actor seamlessly fits their part.

In May 2010, *Udaan* premiered at the Cannes Film Festival—it was the first Indian film to make the official selection after a gap of seven years. That year, the festival emblazoned the names of the directors in official selection on a gigantic banner hoisted across the front of the Palais des Festivals. The name Vikramaditya Motwane stood alongside Jean-Luc Godard (*Film Socialisme*), Mike Leigh (*Another Year*) and Alejandro G. Iñárritu (*Biutiful*). I remember taking photographs of this banner and texting them to Vikram, who had yet to arrive. It was a moment of heart-bursting pride.

You can watch *Udaan* on Netflix India.

42

Vada Chennai

Vada Chennai (Tamil for North Chennai) begins with a shot of a cigarette pack, steel tumblers and a matchbox on a table. A few seconds later, a blood-covered machete is added to the mix. The weapon still has a blob of flesh sticking to it. It looks like freshly kneaded dough. The camera moves wider. We see four men discussing, with the nonchalance of seasoned killers, the consequences of the murder they have just committed.

They are panting, as much from exhaustion as excitement. As the camera circles them, they smoke, plan their next move, and casually wipe blood off their hands. One picks more flesh off his shirt. A few feet away, the dead man lies face down. The killers smile in anticipation of how smoothly the next few decades will go. But a voiceover tells us that this murder will, in fact, haunt them forever.

For the viewer, this opening is the equivalent of being tossed onto a roller coaster mid-plummet. Director-writer Vetri Maaran plunges us into a world of gangsters, rivalry and gore. We don't know the names of these characters yet, but we already have a sense of what they are capable of. The storytelling is so precise that within the first few minutes, we are hooked. What unravels over the next two hours and forty-odd minutes is an epic saga of friendship, betrayal, politics, corruption, romance and revenge. The last, planned meticulously and brewed over decades, is so exquisite that the big reveal will take your breath away.

Released in 2018, *Vada Chennai* is a full-bodied, pulsating portrait of men and women who live hard-scrabble lives in a rough neighbourhood. The magic comes from the fact that Vetri Maaran combines documentary-style starkness with mainstream tropes to deliver a film that is both tough and transporting. But first, you'll have to keep track of the half a dozen characters in pivotal roles. Vetri Maaran helpfully provides a long expository sequence in which one police officer gives another the lay of gangster-land—who is affiliated to whom and which areas each one controls. Still, the film can get confusing, especially if you are not a Tamil speaker.

At the centre of the story is Anbu (which means affection), a wiry young man who is a whiz at carom. Rajan, the top don in their 'hood, introduces Anbu to the sport. He encourages him to use his talent to break the cycle of poverty and crime that afflicts their urban ghetto. But like Michael Corleone in *The Godfather*, Anbu cannot escape his surroundings or his destiny. He becomes embroiled in the dangerous power games being played by Rajan's men—Guna, Senthil, Velu, Muthu—and Rajan's brother, Thambi. It's a dance of death that plays out over years. The film ends on the promise of a sequel, assuring us that the cycle of violence continues.

Vada Chennai is sprawling in its scope and concerns. The film is divided into chapters, with much of the first half set inside a prison. The plot skips back and forth in time, from the late 1980s to the early aughts, weaving a tapestry that is thrilling and tragic. The narrative touches on corruption, dirty politics, the price of development and the displacement of the underprivileged. Amid all this, Vetri Maaran manages to embed two moving love stories: one between Anbu and Padma, and the other between Rajan and Chandra. This might be an overwhelmingly male world, but the women have heft. Padma, who is memorably introduced with a cuss word, and Chandra, played with the right touch of steel by Andrea Jeremiah, have a subtle power. Chandra is a key player in the orchestrated mayhem.

There's an older woman whose distinctive face can be seen in key moments—she prophesies what is to come, suggesting there's a pattern to the seemingly random events. This gives the tale a sense of timelessness and the hint of a larger design in which these men, scrambling and murdering for power, are merely puppets.

Vada Chennai might revolve around the reluctant hero Anbu, but Vetri Maaran doesn't sacrifice the story at the altar of his star and co-producer Dhanush. Instead, he carefully etches each of the other characters so that even the minor ones, like Padma's belligerent father, who isn't keen that she marry Anbu, become memorable. The actors, and there are so many of them, never hit a false note. Ameer as Rajan, Aishwarya Rajesh as Padma, Kishore as Senthil, Samuthirakani as Guna, Pavan as Velu are given their moments in the spotlight without disturbing the painstakingly choreographed narrative. The twists and turns keep coming until the end.

The visuals range from naturalistic to dream-like, but DOP R. Velraj blends the varied tonalities seamlessly. The centrepiece is a wondrous action sequence that takes place in a jail. The bloodlust of men is lit by shafts of sunlight swirling with dust. It's a thing of both horror and beauty. Just like this film.

You can watch *Vada Chennai* on Disney+ Hotstar.

43

Aaranya Kaandam

'*Aaranya*' is Tamil for forest. '*Kaandam*' means chapter. The name is derived from the portion of the Ramayana in which Sita is kidnapped by Raavan. Which may be a reference to the two female characters in the film, both held against their will. Or perhaps director Thiagarajan Kumararaja is alluding to the jungle law that prevails in this unhinged world of gangsters (as with the tilted angles he uses to emphasize the loss of balance).

Or perhaps the name suggests that the characters he has so meticulously created (Thiagarajan is also the writer) are beasts—particularly the two criminal brothers, Gajapathy and Gajendran, both of whom have an imposing physicality, though it's hard to reconcile either with the elephant, who in popular imagination is gentle and wise.

It's not just the title that's a teaser, open to interpretation. *Aaranya Kaandam* (2011) is one of those dense films, peppered with Easter eggs, that provide endless decoding pleasure.

Thiagarajan masterfully blends drama, dark humour, betrayal, violence, sex and pop-culture references. He underlines it all with a flair for storytelling and tops it off with flat-out wackiness. As long as you're in his grip, Thiagarajan makes sure you never lose sight of the fact that the world is essentially a theatre of the absurd.

The film is a groundbreaking debut. It begins with a conversation between Nagadathan and the master strategist Chanakya in 400 BC. Nagadathan asks, 'What is dharma?' Chanakya replies, 'Whatever satiates the need.' The lines, taken from one of Thiagarajan's favourite books, *From Volga to Ganga* (a 1943 collection of short stories by Rahul Sankrityayan), lay the foundation for the amoral landscape that his characters inhabit.

There are no heroes here. Neither is a backstory ever offered to explain why these people are the way they are. Each character is pursuing his or her need and we, the audience, are clearly not meant to pronounce judgement on their actions. After all, the inhabitants of a jungle don't have the luxury of pondering what is right and what is wrong. It is survival not just of the fittest, but of the most devious, the nimblest and the most daring.

The survivors-at-any-cost include Subbu (Yasmin Ponnappa), a young woman who lives with the ageing don Singa Perumal (Jackie Shroff). Perumal is a lion in winter. In the first scene, he is waving a cloth around, trying to kill a fly. He seems curiously ineffectual. He then tries to have sex and fails. The don is at once repulsive and animalistic, intimidating and doddering. Subbu has no option but to submit to his sexual assaults—she once naïvely believed that he was going to make her a film star; now she is trapped like prey. Perumal is impotent. When he can't perform, he beats Subbu. She becomes a constant reminder of his own inadequacy.

Outside the bedroom too, Singa Perumal's prowess is fading. In the next scene, when his top man Pasupathy

(Sampath Raj) suggests they steal a packet of cocaine from the dreaded brothers Gajapathy and Gajendran, Perumal declares it too risky. Pasupathy taunts him, asking, 'Where are your balls?' He adds, 'You've grown old . . . You've lost the guts to run this business.' To which Perumal bares his teeth uncomfortably close to Pasupathy's face. It's like watching two wild animals snarl over territory. Perumal agrees to the deal, perhaps to prove that he hasn't lost his mojo. The cocaine sets in motion a series of events that overturns the power structures of this jungle. It is every man and every woman for themselves—in other words, each fulfilling their dharma.

But *Aaranya Kaandam* is so much more than gangsters running amok. Thiagarajan immerses us in a richly detailed world brimming with colourful characters. There's Sappai (Ravi Krishna), the lowest in the pecking order of Perumal's gang. '*Sappai*' means loser and that's exactly what the others take him to be. When we first meet him, Sappai is serving tea to tougher-looking men as they discuss the most effective ways to seduce a woman. One, named Chittu, gleefully shares that the key is to ask a woman if she is a Kamal Haasan fan or a Rajinikanth fan. If she says Kamal, it will be easy to get her into bed because he oozes sex, Chittu adds.

Sappai can't join the conversation because he's a virgin. Another character turns to him and says, 'Hey loser, why are you such a loser?' Sappai is seen as so ineffectual that Perumal trusts him to keep Subbu company—like Vincent Vega in *Pulp Fiction*, Sappai has to take the boss's wife out. And like Vega, Sappai quickly proves he is no loser.

Thiagarajan consistently toys with our expectations. In one of the most memorable scenes, a 'mind-reading astrologer' walks up to a car in which the manic Gaja brothers are seated and starts talking to Gajendran. It's terrifying because you wonder if the gangster will simply reach over and strangle him, through the open window, with one hand. We know he can, because we've heard Pasupathy tell a story about how Gajendran once bit a woman's thumb off. Our dread rises and then, in an instant, the scene changes tack. The conversation has no bearing on the plot but the situation becomes absurdly funny.

Another story thread follows a father and son, Kaalayan (Guru Soma Sundram) and Kodukapuli (Master Vasanth), who get caught in the crossfire between the gangsters. Kaalayan is royalty on the skids, having drowned his fortune in alcohol. Kodukapuli has an acerbic tongue and zero illusions about the wreck that his father is, but in his gruff manner, you can see signs of affection and loyalty. The bickering between the two is consistently entertaining because Kaalayan, in dirty, tattered clothes, still believes that his lineage entitles him to better treatment and Kodukapuli is smarter and more mature.

Aaranya Kaandam has been described as the first neo-noir Tamil film. It uses the familiar noir tropes: the femme fatale, the voiceover, shadowy lighting, amoral characters. You can see hints of Quentin Tarantino in the crackling rhythm of the dialogue—the casual chatter between the gangsters is a highlight. But Thiagarajan roots his story firmly in north Chennai. The sights, sounds and atmospherics are lived-in and authentic, a case in point being an electrifyingly staged cockfight that leads to more bloodshed.

The background score by Yuvan Shankar Raja has both flamboyance and an almost-existential pathos. The background music includes several songs from other Tamil films—references that were lost on me because I'm not familiar enough with Tamil cinema. But in every instance, the sound enhances the action.

The bloody climax is staged like a confrontation from a Hollywood Western, but the accompanying music, counter-intuitively, is melodic. As throats are sliced and bones broken, its sound stays oddly soothing. The screen is filled with warring men. And then, once again, Thiagarajan delivers a plot twist that upends expectations and cleverly deflates the testosterone display.

Which brings me to Jackie Shroff, who goes out on a limb, playing the impotent don. This is an actor known for his dashing looks, one who has romanced innumerable women on screen. Here, he sheds his vanity along with, sometimes, his clothes—one sequence has him walking around stark naked. Jackie portrays the don's depravity with aplomb. (Apparently he got the role because no actor in the Tamil film industry was willing to do it.)

Some of these scenes aren't in the version of *Aaranya Kaandam* most widely available. The film had a much-publicized run-in with the censors, who demanded fifty-two cuts—even the Kamal versus Rajini joke became a bone of contention. The film was eventually released with an A certificate and several bleeps. The sanitized version can be seen on Disney+ Hotstar, but I would advise you to seek out the uncensored original.

Thiagarajan's exuberant brilliance deserves to be experienced in full.

44

Bandit Queen

David Fincher famously remarked that he was 'interested in movies that scar'. 'The thing I love about *Jaws*,' he said, 'is the fact that I've never gone swimming in the ocean again.'

In my personal pantheon of Films that Scar, *Bandit Queen* is at number one. Shekhar Kapur's unflinching depiction of the life of one of India's most famous dacoits, Phoolan Devi, constituted its own genre: reality as horror. One scene, with a door creaking open and shut as more men walked in to rape Phoolan, kept me up at night. It was like peering into the heart of darkness.

Did it happen like this? *Bandit Queen*, which premiered to critical acclaim at the Cannes Film Festival in 1994, became a landmark in Indian cinema for its portrayal of India's deeply entrenched patriarchal and caste systems. But the film was also a hotbed of controversy. For starters, Phoolan herself disputed Shekhar's version of events, saying the narrative, based on Mala Sen's book, *India's Bandit Queen: The True Story of Phoolan Devi,* was false and exploitative. She went to court demanding a ban, but later settled with the producers (Channel 4) and withdrew her objections.

Author and activist Arundhati Roy, who supported Phoolan and encouraged her to sue, wrote an impassioned two-part essay titled 'The Great Indian Rape Trick', in which she denounced the film, asking how Shekhar could claim to be telling a true story when he hadn't even bothered to meet his subject once. 'There's a sort of loutish arrogance at work here,' she wrote, 'a dunce's courage. Unafraid of what it doesn't know.'

The film, which features cuss words, violence, brutal rape sequences and full-frontal nudity, also ran into trouble with the censor board, sparking a battle that went all the way to the Supreme Court (eventually, the SC upheld the Film Certification Appellate Tribunal's ruling that these elements were necessary). The court ruled that 'A film that carries the message that the social evil is evil cannot be made impermissible on the ground that it depicts the social evil.' In a 2018 *Mint* article, producer Bobby Bedi called this 'a landmark judgement in terms of censorship even today'. He said, 'If I had made the film today, I would have no hopes of getting the same judgement.'

It's impossible to ascertain how much of *Bandit Queen* is fact and how much embellishment. Phoolan's life, as we know it, is a knot of reality, folklore and myth, which has become even harder to detangle after her murder in 2014. The film offers one interpretation, which is arguably limiting, simplistic and even problematic, but as a work of art, *Bandit Queen* endures. Shekhar created a harrowing portrait of a woman who survives unspeakable violence but refuses to be a victim. Instead, she rises and unleashes bloody revenge on her tormentors. Phoolan, with a red band across her forehead and defiant eyes, becomes the ultimate avenging angel.

The film opens on her at age eleven. She's playing in the river with her friends while her father finalizes her marriage to someone who, in exchange, will give him a cow and a bicycle. After a perfunctory wedding ceremony, she is pushed out of the house. The close-up, of a little girl with *sindoor* in her hair, is at once grotesque and heartbreaking. Phoolan's thirty-three-year-old husband forces her to have sex with him. When she keels over in pain and cannot do the chores, he threatens he'll do it again. It's horrific, and the film offers no relief or diversion. Phoolan's world is casually violent, consistently unjust. In terms of status, she is barely at par with the cow she was traded for. But Phoolan, who even at that age is fierce, refuses to make her peace with that. She leaves her husband and returns home.

As she grows into adulthood, the boys in the village start to harass her. When she rebuffs the upper-caste *sarpanch*'s son, she is made to leave the village. She ends up in the hands of bandits and eventually becomes one. Her life becomes the stuff of legend—she is a *devi*, a Robin Hood-style rebel who roams the Chambal ravines. But she is also a murderer. In one scene, her lover and fellow gang leader Vikram Mallah tells her, 'If you are going to kill, kill twenty, not one. If you kill twenty, you will be famous. If you kill only one, they will hang you.'

Phoolan, who is as shrewd as she is strong, understands this slippery connection between notoriety and survival. A turning point in the film is the Behmai massacre in 1981, in which Phoolan and her men kill twenty Thakur men. This was, as the *Atlantic* magazine reported in a 1996 article titled 'India's Bandit Queen', 'the largest dacoit massacre since the founding of modern India. And it was triply shocking: because of its scale, because it was led by a woman, and because a woman of lower caste murdered men of a vastly higher one.' Even after the massacre, Phoolan managed to evade capture for two years. The film ends with her surrender in 1983.

Bandit Queen is a tough story rendered with quiet poetry. The film was shot by one of Hindi cinema's great cinematographers, Ashok Mehta. His lens captures the arid beauty of the vast, dusty landscape that shelters the dacoits. They loot and kill and disappear into the steep ravines like snakes into their burrows. Mehta also captures the striking beauty of Seema Biswas, who plays Phoolan. Seema didn't look like the heroines of the day— her desirability wasn't located in fair skin, big eyes, a svelte body or lustrous hair. She exuded strength. The role required her to enact scenes that had never been seen in a Hindi film before, and she delivered. In one, Phoolan, now a dreaded dacoit, goes back to her husband's village, parades him around it on a donkey and then almost beats him to death with her rifle. The rage and hurt on her face will make your hair stand on end. It feels like a scene from Judgment Day, with Phoolan avenging every woman who has ever been abused by a man.

Seema, who was discovered by Shekhar at the National School of Drama (NSD) repertory, embodied the complex and contradictory layers of Phoolan: her indomitable spirit and her aching vulnerability, her mischievousness and her overwhelming tragedy. It's a brilliant performance that won the actress a National Award. *Bandit Queen* was peppered with newcomers like her who delivered like thespians, many of them also from the NSD: Nirmal Pandey who plays Vikram Mallah; Manoj Bajpayee, making his feature film debut as Man Singh, Phoolan's confidante after Vikram dies; Govind Namdeo who plays Phoolan's terrifying nemesis Shri Ram; Saurabh Shukla, wonderful as her supportive cousin Kailash. Interestingly, *Bandit Queen* is generally acknowledged as the first Hindi film to have a casting director—Tigmanshu Dhulia, who later went on to direct his own celebrated bandit film, *Paan Singh Tomar*.

Bandit Queen was edited by Renu Saluja, a formidable artist who ensured that, despite its documentary-style realism, the film had the pace and grip of a drama. The soundtrack by Nusrat Fateh Ali Khan added to the haunting lyricism of the visuals.

Bandit Queen is overpowering but also empowering. It's a tough sit, but it rips the curtain away to reveal the horrors of caste and gender violence in our country; sadly, the narrative of injustice and abuse remains relevant.

The film is available on YouTube and MX Player. But this isn't a film to be seen with the cuss words bleeped out or commercial interruptions. Find an untouched version and prepare to be immersed in the hellish reality of a low-caste rural Indian woman. This one happened to hit back.

45

Celluloid Man

Sometime before he started shooting for Satyajit Ray's *Shatranj Ke Khilari* (1977), Sanjeev Kumar lived in Poona (now Pune) for a month, and spent every evening at the National Film Archive of India (NFAI), watching Ray films. Kumar, a celebrated Hindi film star, had heard of the maestro but had never seen his cinema. He was embarrassed to show up without having done his homework.

P.K. Nair, erstwhile director of the NFAI, tells this story with admiration for the actor and his commitment. With typical modesty, he forgets to add that the only reason Sanjeev Kumar could study Ray with such ease was because Nair devoted his life to collecting, preserving and promulgating film. This he did in a country that cares so little about the art of archiving that we do not even have one surviving print of India's first talkie, *Alam Ara* (1931).

Nair built up the archive through sheer, obstinate, unrelenting passion. His was the sort of single-minded obsession that compels one to neglect family and sacrifice health and comfort. *Celluloid Man* (2012), a documentary by director Shivendra Singh Dungarpur, is the moving portrait of this man, who single-handedly tracked down and cared for large swathes of India's cinematic history.

Nair Saab, as he was affectionately called, was a ferocious movie warrior. He battled bureaucratic politics, apathetic and ignorant filmmakers and nightmarish logistical hurdles to find films and archive them. He was, every inch and in every waking breath, a celluloid man.

Archiving has never been a priority for the Indian film industry. Preservation mattered so little to the businessmen who made India's earliest movies that once the profits were in, the inconvenient reels of highly inflammable nitrate were discarded, tossed in cans and forgotten, or sold to be stripped for silver and used to make bangles. It is estimated that 1,700 silent feature films were made in India between 1913 and 1932. Most of these are gone forever. In one of the documentary's most poignant moments, Nair recalls director Ardeshir Irani's son telling him that he disposed of the *Alam Ara* reels himself, after extracting the silver from them.

The NFAI was formally established in February 1964. Nair was its curator and then its first director, but his job was akin to that of an archaeologist excavating at an ancient ruin. Months of labour would sometimes yield treasure but often lead nowhere. Nair relives his efforts to find *Raja Harishchandra*, India's first feature, made by the pioneering Dhundiraj Govind aka Dadasaheb Phalke. Nair contacted Phalke's daughter, then travelled from Poona to Nasik, to Phalke's house, where he was rewarded with a wooden box that held stray reels of various Phalke films, a notebook on shots, presumably written by Phalke, and most of one of Phalke's most famous films, *Kaliya Mardan* (1919). There were also two reels from *Raja Harishchandra*.

Nair's adventures took him to remote parts of the country. He searched wherever the clues led him, sometimes in cowsheds and godowns. Critically, Nair did not discriminate. The quality of a film did not determine its importance. He saw all film as cultural artefact. And so the NFAI preserved for posterity Ray's films as well as the action entertainers starring Fearless Nadia, India's first action heroine, each providing a view of the world as it once was.

Nair's legacy isn't just the invaluable collection at the NFAI (in the compilation of his writings, *Yesterday's Films for Tomorrow*, he writes that the archive had approximately 12,000 titles by the time he retired in 1991). It is also the generations of directors he unwittingly tutored. Through the seventies and eighties, students at the Film and Television Institute of India (FTII) were beneficiaries of Nair's largesse. He encouraged and enabled them to watch as many films as they could from the archive. *Celluloid Man* features a slew of famous faces who speak of the impact that Nair had on their lives: Ketan Mehta, Jahnu Barua, Girish Kasaravalli, Naseeruddin Shah, Jaya Bachchan (then Bhaduri) and my husband Vinod, who recalls that Nair loaned him a print of Jean-Luc Godard's *Breathless* so that he could study the editing pattern.

But my favourite anecdote comes from filmmaker-cinematographer Venu. He tells of how the avant-garde Malayalam filmmaker John Abraham once woke Nair at 3 a.m. and demanded to see Pier Paolo Pasolini's *The Gospel According to St Matthew*. Nair didn't grumble or hesitate. He headed to the vault, took the film out and summoned the projectionist. He and Abraham then watched the film until dawn and spent another few hours discussing Abraham's upcoming film.

Celluloid Man is suffused with nostalgia and melancholy. The film begins with Nair returning to the NFAI after eleven years (the frame looks like something from a Guru Dutt film).

His forthright manner had alienated the powers that were and the man who had built the edifice was once barred from entering it. As Nair walks through the spaces (his old office is now a storage room filled with boxes) and the film vaults, picking up cans and rattling off reel numbers for specific film sequences, there is an ineffable sense of loss. For Nair, whose brilliant work is ultimately at the mercy of bureaucrats who lack his missionary zeal and vision. And for film itself—it is heartbreaking to see spools lying neglected on cobwebbed shelves.

But Shivendra also infuses a touch of mischief. One of Nair's heroes was the legendary Henri Langlois, the co-founder of the Cinematheque Francaise archive in Paris. Langlois, also a cinema warrior, used to add to the Cinematheque's collection by making unauthorized duplicates (dupes) of international classics that were sent to Paris for special screenings. Nair did the same. When Shivendra asks him about this 'piracy', Nair sheepishly replies, 'A true archivist should have immunity.'

A true archivist should also have, if not stardom, at least recognition. Nair died in March 2016. Shivendra, a leading archivist himself, has played a critical role in preserving the memory of the man and his contribution to our national heritage. For a lover of Indian cinema, *Celluloid Man* is essential viewing. An added attraction are the clips from a few of the treasures he saved—among them *Kaliya Mardan*, *Kismet* (1943) and *Chandralekha* (1948). Thanks to Nair Saab, these classics remain with us.

You can watch *Celluloid Man* on Mubi India.

46

Chalti Ka Naam Gaadi

Late on a rainy night, a car breaks down. The lone passenger, a woman, sees a garage nearby. Drenched and shivering, she knocks on the door. There's no response. In desperation, she pounds on it several times. A man finally appears.

If this were a contemporary film, the situation would be suspenseful, sexual, or perhaps the start of a horror movie. But in 1958, this constituted the setting of one of the greatest meet-cutes in Hindi cinema.

Manu the mechanic first tries to send Renu away. He wants to go back to sleep. He thinks she is a *museebat*. But when she pleads for help, he helps her push the car into the garage and starts to work on it. He offers her tea, which she declines. And then, as he tinkers beneath the hood, to lift her foul mood, he sings the delightful '*Ek Ladki Bheegi Bhagi Si*'. S.D. Burman's song with Majrooh Sultanpuri's lyrics is so lilting and mischievous that over half a century later, DJs are still playing remixed versions in nightclubs. We know that, sooner rather than later, Renu will succumb to Manu's eccentric charm.

Exuberance is the operating principle of *Chalti Ka Naam Gaadi*. The film has three real-life brothers—Ashok, Kishore and Anoop Kumar—playing the brothers Birju, Manu and Jaggu, who own and operate the Mohan Brothers Garage. They live together, work together and sometimes even wear the same clothes (think of them as the cinematic ancestors of the real-life Burmawalla brothers, directors Abbas and Mustan, and editor Hussain, who dressed in identical white clothes, and together created blockbusters such as *Khiladi*, *Baazigar* and the *Race* franchise).

In one pivotal scene, Birju, Jaggu and Manu are wearing matching striped night suits and eating dinner. Manu is in a funk because Renu is upset with him. As the eldest, Birju, advises Manu to stay away from women. Jaggu tries to make peace by echoing Birju. The scene is sombre—Manu is troubled and, for the first time, is questioning Birju's anti-women stance. And yet director Satyen Bose manages to inflect the scene with humour. Even the beat of the dialogue provides laughs—the conversation ricochets between the three like a ping-pong ball. You wonder if real-life dinners at the Kumar household were anything like this.

Chalti Ka Naam Gaadi was conceived of by Kishore Kumar (who was reportedly a fan of the Marx Brothers comedies). Bose, who was roped in at the last minute after director Kamal Majumdar exited the project, was credited with directing the film, but it is widely believed that the creative reins remained in the hands of Kishore Kumar.

Whatever the case, the casting was inspired. Ashok Kumar as the champion boxer Birju has an easy authority. Birju hates women (we discover why later in the film). He wants to shield his brothers from heartbreak, so he enforces a blanket ban: even posters of women aren't allowed in the garage. Anoop Kumar, as the middle brother Jaggu, makes a terrific buffer—the hapless Jaggu mediates between his two more domineering brothers by agreeing with both. And the masterstroke is Kishore Kumar as Manu. The singer-actor-composer-director-producer-writer was also a masterful funny man. His onscreen personality was inherently comedic—even straight-faced and standing still, he could make you smile. Kishore Kumar makes Manu so gloriously goofy and endearing that you never question how Renu, rich, beautiful and successful, could have fallen in love with the garage mechanic. The clincher is that he makes her laugh (even in a supposedly serious scene in which they are chasing the bad guy), and what woman can resist that?

Renu is also a singular sensation. For one thing, she's played by Madhubala, whose luminous beauty is more pronounced in black-and-white—perhaps because there is less to distract us from her face. For another, Renu is independent (she is a dancer, though we never see her perform) and she has agency—she propels their relationship, going to Manu's house, taking him out on a date (they go on a picnic). He has far more familial restrictions than she does. Renu's hobbies are 'riding, swimming and motor driving' and she is also braver than Manu. When they are in precarious situations, he mostly just repeats her name, saying 'Renu, Renu, Renu' (which is hilarious). She's the one with the plan.

Which comes in handy because they are up against the conniving Raja Hardayal Singh, played by K.N. Singh with a single curl arranged artfully on his forehead. K.N. Singh was one of Hindi cinema's most civilized baddies. He brought a studied sophistication to his villainy—here, he first appears dressed in a suit and bowtie, and later can be seen conniving while draped in a silken dressing gown. The Raja is interested in Renu for her money and concocts a twisted scheme to get at it. Of course, Renu and Manu foil his dastardly plan.

Chalti Ka Naam Gaadi includes a murder and a character who has been abused and imprisoned, but Bose and his writers, Ramesh Pant and Govind Moonis, don't let these dark notes overwhelm the film's raison d'être: to make you laugh. Even the titles—animated sketches that reflect the credit on screen—serve this aim. So 'Produced by' appears with the sketch of a nurse carrying a baby in a maternity ward and 'Directed by' features a policeman directing a car, which hits a pole. All of this is set to a lively medley of the songs in the film.

S.D. Burman's brilliant music ratchets up the effervescence: the film begins with the three brothers in their car, a 1928 jalopy named Champion, singing '*Babu Samjho Ishare*' as they race down the wide and relatively unpopulated roads of Bombay. This first sequence sets the tone of joyous zaniness, which never falters. Even if you watch just a couple of the songs—'*Main Sitaron Ka Tarana*' or '*Hum They Voh Thi*'—you'll come away smiling.

Comedy rarely gets the respect it deserves. In the 1941 Hollywood film *Sullivan's Travels*, director Preston Sturges tells the story of a successful film director, John Sullivan, who has earned fame and riches making comedies, but now wants to make a serious film, or as he puts it, 'a picture with dignity'. Since he knows little about the lives of the downtrodden, he becomes a hobo and embarks on a journey to experience hardship. His travels eventually lead him to appreciate the value of comedy. He says, 'There's a lot to be said for making people laugh. Did you know that that's all some people have? It isn't much, but it's better than nothing in this cock-eyed caravan.'

Chalti Ka Naam Gaadi works like a strong shot of optimism and cheer. You can watch the film on YouTube.

47

Daayraa

A woman has been raped and is weeping. In the manner of dozens of Hindi film heroines before her, she wails, '*Meri izzat loot li.*' The man listening to her scoffs and replies, '*Ek zara sa chamdi ka tukda izzat kaise ho sakta hai? Bhagwan itna bewakoof nahin ki izzat wahan rakhega.*' He touches her forehead and adds, '*Yahan hoti hai izzat—mastak mein.*'

This is a scene from *Daayraa* (1996), directed by Amol Palekar and written by the novelist and playwright Timeri N. Murari. The word '*daayraa*' means boundary. The film is an ode to the flouting of restrictions: of sex, gender, society, patriarchy. The idea of a love story between a trans-woman and a woman who is forced to dress like a man was so groundbreaking at the time that the film was never released theatrically in India. *Daayraa* was given the 'A' certification on 'thematic value', which meant that it would have a limited audience in theatres and couldn't be shown on television either.

Leading distributors saw it but deemed it unviable. Eventually the producer, Pravesh Sippy, decided to focus his energies on taking the film abroad, where it was released as *The Square Circle*. Until then, there had never been a Hindi film like *Daayraa*. There hasn't been one since.

The story is set in Odisha. Nirmal Pandey plays a classically trained dancer who cross-dresses and performs as a woman in a touring theatre. As women begin to enter the profession, he becomes obsolete. But this is his identity, so he remains in his female avatar and becomes a sort of wandering minstrel who roams the land, entertaining with music and drama. On this journey, he meets a young woman, played by Sonali Kulkarni, who has been kidnapped by a brothel madam on the eve of her wedding. She runs away but is attacked and raped by goons. The woman and the dancer befriend each other. The dancer convinces her to dress like a man, telling her that's the only way she will be safe. They travel together as a couple, and slowly their relationship blossoms into love.

It's revealing that we never find out the names of these two individuals. The dancer describes themself as a '*kudrat ka karishma*'. You get the sense that this is a life so free that even a name would be a limitation. The runaway too sheds conventional ideas of propriety and the notions of marriage and romance that she once clung to. As the two roam the country, she learns to fend for herself, comes into her own and, as the dancer tells her, becomes 'a brave woman like I was'.

Murari's script redefines masculinity. The most awful characters on screen are the men. The goons who kidnap the woman; the other goons who rape her as if that's part of the entertainment—they are drinking, riding their motorcycles, and she becomes an opportunity for more pleasure; her father and husband-to-be who reject her when she returns to her village, because she is now 'tainted'. In this toxic landscape, the hero is this dancer, who comforts her and provides support—in one scene, the dancer is a maternal figure, singing her a lullaby as she rests her head on their lap.

The film ridicules the behaviour considered socially acceptable in men. In one scene, the dancer takes the woman, now dressed as a man, to a bar and encourages her to drink. When she throws up, the dancer says, *'Yeh hui na, mardon wali baat.'*

The dancer is a fascinating character, who lives a hard life but refuses to complain and has no patience with the woman's self-pity either. The morning after she is raped, the woman is staring at a knife. The dancer has just offered her breakfast. When she stalls, the dancer casually says, *'Khayegi ya khudkhushi karegi . . . jo karna hai jaldi tay kar.'*

The dancer revels in putting on saris, jewellery and make-up. Nirmal Pandey plays this character with finesse and empathy. He revels in the dancer's grace and delicacy as a woman. In one scene, we see him putting on a bra. It is a brave performance, especially for a Hindi film actor in the nineties.

The film also attempts to break cinematic boundaries— Palekar tries to construct a hybrid work that combines art-house content and mainstream tropes. The film uses folk music and lip-synced songs, composed by Anand-Milind and written by Gulzar. The choreography is by Saroj Khan. But the blend isn't entirely successful. *Daayraa* suffers from sloppy editing, clumsily staged action sequences (especially the rape scenes) and bizarre detours. At one point, the two main characters spend the night in the home of a young widow who tries to persuade the woman, who is dressed like a man, to have sex with her. The scene ends with the widow dousing herself with cold water. It plays as comical rather than wrenching (though even here the film was progressive enough to acknowledge that a widow could have sexual desires).

The daring subversions in story make it possible to ignore the lapses in craft. *Daayraa* won a National Award and made it to *Time* magazine's list of the ten best films of the year. In 2015, the film was released on DVD.

I don't know if it's easily available, but if you make the effort to find *Daayraa*, you will be surprised and moved by this bittersweet road movie. It is, like its key character, one of a kind.

48

Diljit Dosanjh

Nobody knows anything, Oscar-winning screenwriter William Goldman famously declared of the movie business. A fine example of this truism is the career of Punjabi sensation Diljit Dosanjh.

Conventional wisdom dictates that Diljit should, at best, be a local singing star. When his first Punjabi film, *The Lion of Punjab* (2011), flopped, he was categorically told that even the Punjab audience wasn't willing to accept a turbaned hero. But through sheer grit and industrial-strength charm, the man has fashioned a blazing acting career in both Punjabi and Hindi cinema, done concerts in sold-out stadiums around the world and become a social media sensation, with millions following his funny, self-deprecating posts, which record his globe-trotting life (Diljit in the kitchen, experimenting with new recipes, has its own fan base). He's the closest I've come to witnessing a showbiz Cinderella story.

We first met in April 2016, before the release of his first Hindi film, *Udta Punjab*. I had recently seen his 2014 film,

Punjab 1984, the story of a mother searching for her son who has gone missing during the violence of the anti-Sikh riots. Diljit's performance made a big impression. I reached out to the film's director, Anurag Singh, and asked if he could make an introduction. We set up an interview.

Diljit and I didn't speak the same language; he is most comfortable in Punjabi and I in English. And yet we managed to communicate, chatting for almost an hour about his incredible journey, his excitement at working with Kareena Kapoor in *Udta Punjab*, and his desperate desire to own a pair of Adidas Yeezy 350s. At one point, he made a direct-to-camera plea to rapper-designer Kanye West, saying, 'Kim Kardashian *ke* husband, *jab* shoes *banaate ho*, don't make them out of stock, *do logon ko.*' I had never heard of the coveted Yeezys and it took me a few minutes to figure out that this impassioned speech was about sneakers.

What was immediately apparent was Diljit's candour and authenticity. He wasn't reticent about his background (he comes from a village near Jalandhar) or his inability to speak English. He didn't seem intimidated by the Hindi film industry, which can be an alienating place for outsiders. Diljit confidently owned his persona of the 'urban *pendu*'. The word '*pendu*' comes from '*pind*', meaning village. In the video for his song, '*Proper Patola*', Diljit wears a sweatshirt that says 'Urban Pendu'. When I asked him how close he was to being this, he smiled and said, '*Pendu toh main hoon*, urban *thoda* wannabe *hai.*'

That seamless mix of earthy and edgy has defined Diljit's persona, his brand and his sense of style. At our first interview, he wore unflashy grey tracks and a white shirt—the only standout statement was a pink *pagdi*. But by the time we did our second interview, in July 2018, the fashion maven in him had blossomed. His sartorial choices were making news: he was featured on the pages of the Indian edition of *GQ* magazine. The evening of our second meeting, Diljit wore a strikingly colourful Gucci shirt. When I asked him about this evolving sense of style, he said he'd always had it, he just hadn't had the money to indulge it. A year later, Diljit made the cover of *Vogue India* wearing a baggy pink blazer and red track pants, standing next to Kareena Kapoor Khan, Natasha Poonawalla and Karan Johar, with a headline that read 'Forces of Fashion'. Inside, however, the magazine only carried three interviews— Diljit left because the reporter was asking questions in rapid-fire English.

Diljit redefined the Bollywood hero. And it wasn't just the turban. It was also his disarming, wide-eyed, son-of-the-soil appeal, a sharp contrast to the urbane, gym-chiselled leading men that crowd the Hindi film industry. In 2017, he played the lead opposite Anushka Sharma in *Phillauri*, a comedy about a ghost. At one point, we see him shirtless, bathing at a tube well. As Karanjeet Kaur, writing in *Arre*, put it, 'When has a Sikh man in mainstream Hindi cinema been considered an object of desire? When has his body been sexualised?' Diljit turned 'urban *pendu*' into a legitimate brand.

In 2019, Diljit became the first turbaned Sikh to have a wax statue at Madame Tussauds. He's been brand ambassador for Coca-Cola and Tissot. Through the years and successes, the externals—clothes, cars, videos—got swankier, but the man seemed to stay the same. In posts on social media, he was still as excited about luxurious hotel rooms and private planes; he still struggled with English; and he still, somehow, seamlessly combined Punjabi popstar swag with the humility of an ingenu. In 2020, he released an album called *G.O.A.T* (the acronym for Greatest of All Time) but insisted, in an interview, that he was far from being that. Only the legend Gurdas Maan deserves that epithet, he added.

In one of our many interviews, Diljit said, '*Saaf niyat se jo banda mehnat karta hai toh kudrat usko deti hi hai, yeh toh niyam hai.*' In the hyper-competitive, brutally Darwinian world of showbiz, '*saaf niyat*' sounds like a feeble weapon. And yet it seems to have worked for Diljit. He is an outlier but his career is proof that sincerity, talent and rigour can trump gargantuan odds. For me, his journey has been a continual source of joy and inspiration.

Among Diljit's many ambitions is doing a film in Hollywood. Which of course seems impossible. But watching him soar has taught me to never say never. With Diljit, there is always hope that yet another mountain will be conquered.

49

Guide

'Zindagi bhi ek nasha hai dost. Jab chadhta hai poocho mat kya alam rehta hai, lekin jab utarta hai . . .'

These words are uttered by Raju, the guide, in Vijay Anand's 1965 classic *Guide*. Raju is drinking with his assistant Mani, whom he has cajoled into keeping him company. They are sitting in a lavish bungalow but Raju is sad and desperately lonely. The intoxication of love, success, money and fame is slowly seeping out of his life. Upstairs, Rosie, for whom he fought with his mother, his closest friend and his neighbours, lies alone in her bed, with her door bolted. The distance between them seems unbridgeable.

This is one of the many haunting sequences in the film, which remains remarkable for its narrative complexity and the way in which it explores the tension between art, worldly success and spirituality. *Guide*, adapted from a 1958 novel by R.K. Narayan, is about the doomed love between two flawed people—Raju is charming, loving, generous, but he's also manipulative, a bit of a charlatan and willing to live off Rosie's success as a dancer. He is the key architect of her rise to glory, but the rush of money and power throws him off-balance. Rosie is strong and fiercely talented, but also blows cold, and pushes Raju away when he needs her most. In one of the most beautiful love songs in Hindi cinema, *'Tere Mere Sapne'*, they promise each other eternal love: *'laakh manaa le duniya, saath naa yeh chhutega / aake tere haathon mein haath naa yeh chhutega'*. But their bond splinters as their fortunes rise.

Guide was remarkably forward for its time. Rosie is married when she falls in love with Raju. Vijay Anand, who also wrote the Hindi screenplay and dialogue, doesn't tiptoe around this. Instead, he shows us the sham that is her marriage: her husband Marco is cruel, uncaring and adulterous. An archaeologist, he is more interested in the caves and statues that he discovers with Raju's help than he is in his wife. He also disrespects her art. In fact, he kicks the tabla in anger when he discovers her dancing in their house. Raju is the opposite. He encourages Rosie to hone her talent. He pushes her artistry out into the world and tells her, *'Kalakaar bhaand nahin hote hain.'* When she denigrates herself as a *kalankani* or disreputable person, he simply says, *'Agar tum kalankani toh kalank sar akhon par.'* And yet, they cannot make the relationship work.

Rosie is one of my favourite Hindi film heroines. She's courageous yet vulnerable, ambitious yet afraid, and she's tough enough to walk out on Marco. In one of the film's most dramatic scenes, staged in a darkened cave, Rosie confronts her husband. She is dressed in in her dance finery and wearing the *ghungroos* that he despises so much. Infuriated by her defiance, he lashes out at her but she doesn't retreat. She leaves with her head held high.

Rosie is the daughter of a *devadasi*. Her mother makes her marry Marco so she can lead a better life. In anger, Marco once says that he 'bought' her only to satisfy his needs. Marco is a rich, successful man. Rosie is a dependent woman with a troubled background. But there is never any doubt about who has the real strength and moral high ground here.

Waheeda Rehman embodies every aspect of Rosie. When she sings '*Aaj Phir Jeene Ki Tamanna Hai*' with exuberant abandon, she captures the freedom and unfettered joy that every woman longs for. Her beauty, acting prowess and incredible dancing skills fleshed Rosie into three dimensions. Dev Anand, minimizing his signature mannerisms, matched her at every turn. Raju is a role that actors might dream of—a character that undergoes a 180-degree arc, evolving from a small-town guide to a boozing, gambling big shot to a fake *sadhu* and eventually to someone who has spiritual heft and an understanding of what really matters in life. Raju sacrifices himself for the villagers who have looked after him. He finds his true calling. Raju is hero, villain, saviour, and Dev Anand plumbs the depths of each facet.

The other lead in the film is S.D. Burman's music, with lyrics by Shailendra Singh. *Guide's* is arguably Hindi cinema's finest and most iconic soundtrack. Each song, from '*Wahan Kaun Hai Tera*' (sung by S.D. himself) to the twin tunes '*Mose Chhal Kiye Jaaye*' (Lata Mangeshkar) and '*Kya Se Kya Ho Gaya*' (Mohammed Rafi), is a tour de force. The range is astounding—from love to heartbreak to betrayal to life philosophy, there is a song to echo every sentiment. The tunes are remarkable and the lyrics, profound. Consider the following lines from '*Wahan Kaun Hai Tera*': '*Kehte hain gyaani duniya hai faani / paani pe likhi likhayi / hai sabki dekhi, hai sabki jaani / haath kisi ke na aayi, haath kisi ke na aayi / kuch tera na mera, kuch tera na mera / musafir jaayega kahan*'. Or the boldness with which Vijay Anand positioned '*Mose Chhal Kiye Jaaye*' (in which Rosie expresses her heartache) back-to-back with '*Kya Se Kya Ho Gaya*' (in which

Raju expresses his sadness at the souring of their love). You can see the confidence of a master at work.

Guide is the crown jewel in the Vijay Anand-Dev Anand oeuvre. The brothers risked their money and reputation on an unconventional story. Incredibly, the film was also made in English as *The Guide*. In fact, the English version, written by Pearl S. Buck and directed by Ted Danielewski, was shot before the Hindi one. Buck actually tutored Waheeda Rehman on her English diction. *The Guide* speaks to Dev Anand's ambition: he attempted a crossover decades before the word was coined. The English film was a massive disappointment. The Hindi one also underperformed. Writer R.K. Narayan didn't approve of either version. But over the decades, the Hindi *Guide* found an audience and critical acclaim. Even those born generations after it released know—through its songs—this singularly aching take on love.

In his autobiography, *Romancing with Life*, Dev Anand writes that 'all great works of art are born out of madness'. *Guide* certainly attests to that.

The film is available on DVD.

50

Aditya Chopra

Greta Garbo-style stardom is largely extinct in contemporary Bollywood. Few artists believe in the strategic advantage of keeping a low profile and maintaining an aura of mystery in order to sustain audience interest. Social media demands incessant sharing. And the advertorial model of entertainment news (popularly known as medianet) enables anyone with money to buy prime space in the press. Fame is no longer the by-product of your art. Being famous has become an art in itself. Celebrity is a bona fide goal.

In this environment, Aditya Chopra stands out like a dinosaur. He is a powerful artist who chooses to remain invisible. The elder son of Yash Chopra, Aditya heads Yash Raj Films. He was also the director of *Dilwale Dulhania Le Jayenge*, the longest-running film in the history of Indian cinema. Aditya is married to Rani Mukerji. He could easily find ways to be in the news every week. But few people know what he looks like—even the photos of him on the Internet are several years old. When actors thank him in their awards acceptance speeches, they routinely joke that he is not a myth, that he actually exists. Aditya's fiercely guarded privacy is like his oxygen—he can't live without it. He is Hindi cinema's resident hermit.

This reclusiveness is not a response to the current bare-all, share-all environment. It was in place when he was a newbie, cutting trailers for his father. I first met Aditya in 1993. My mother, Kamna Chandra, had written the original story of Yashji's *Chandni*. Her work and relationship with the family took us occasionally to the sprawling Chopra bungalow in suburban Mumbai. On one such visit, Aditya showed me the trailer he had made for *Darr*, his father's film, which was going to release soon. The trailer was Aditya's first act of disruption. Back then, there was little idea of marketing a film beyond hoardings, and no one invested the time and care to create television trailers. But Aditya put together a compelling promo that teased the audience with glimpses of the unhinged lover, the beauteous woman he was obsessed with, and the woman's tough-as-nails husband, whom he must eventually battle. It was a potent cocktail; later, a leading director remarked that it was, in fact, better than the film.

I was then a journalist for *India Today* magazine. I was writing a story on the new artistic voices on the horizon and was keen to feature Aditya in it. *DDLJ* hadn't released yet but I was convinced Adi, as people in the business call him, was going to be trailblazer. Aditya agreed. But just as the photographer and I were getting ready to leave our office in south Mumbai to head to the Yash Raj office in the suburbs, the landline rang. It was Aditya. He told me he just wasn't comfortable with media attention. He was deeply apologetic but resolute in his determination to remain hidden. He didn't want fame, even before he had it.

This did not change. Aditya became a power player but refused to engage with the publicity machinery. In 2001, the British Film Institute commissioned me to write a book on *DDLJ* as part of their Modern Classics series. After much begging and cajoling, Aditya eventually agreed to participate. And once he started to speak, it was like a dam had burst. Listening to him talk, for hours, about how he created an iconic film at twenty-four has been one of the great joys of my career.

Aditya is a nation builder, but his nation is his cinema. I remember doing an interview with Yashji a little after *DDLJ* became a blockbuster. I asked him what Aditya might want to do next. Yashji said Aditya didn't care about clothes or cars. All he wanted was a studio. That studio became a reality and a young man with an outsized vision created a home for a legion of directors, actors, technicians. Aditya also set up his own overseas distribution company, publicity department and music label. You could, if you liked, walk into Yash Raj Films with a script and walk out with a finished film.

I've always wondered how Aditya's retreat from public life feeds his vision. Does the lack of noise and distraction allow him to create with more freedom and flourish? For years now, he's followed the practice of watching films 'first day, first show' in a cinema hall. During my interviews for the *DDLJ* book, Aditya explained it like this: 'The purity of *DDLJ* came because I see films for just the love of films. I love films and the charm of going to the theatre, buying a ticket, buying popcorn and waiting for the film to start—that is my greatest high. Nothing gives me more pleasure than that. It is largely responsible for the kind of film I made. It gives me a lot of respect for the audience. I never want to fake an emotion or cheat them. I can only be sincere when I am one of the audience. I firmly believe that if I cannot sit in the theatre as a common person, I'll be finished.'

Aditya's anonymity gives him a direct line to the audience. But this doesn't mean that all his films work—some YRF productions have been monstrous clunkers, like *Thugs of Hindostan* and *Befikre*, which Aditya directed himself. And yet, this umbilical chord is an advantage. And in a notoriously unpredictable business, it's a lifeline worth fighting for.

51

The Cannes Film Festival

In May 2008, I walked the red carpet at the Cannes Film
Festival for the first time. This sixty-metre strip is perhaps the
world's most scrutinized and publicized real-estate after the
Oscars red carpet. The Cannes red carpet leads to the Grand
Theatre Lumiere, a stunning, cavernous space that seats over
two thousand people. This is where the competition films are
screened. Hundreds of people line up to cheer the artists, who
descend from swanky cars emblazoned with the festival logo.
On either side of the carpet are rows of photographers, in
tuxedoes, who capture the dazzle and disseminate the pictures
to far corners of the world. This stretch captures perfectly
the delicious cocktail of artistry, glamour and business that
is Cannes.

I first attended the festival in 1999, as a correspondent
for *India Today* magazine. The festival's singular frenzy was
palpable—when 30,000-odd people gather in a tiny resort town
to celebrate, showcase and market cinema, the buzz is electric.

It's also intimidating. The festival is labyrinthine, and I spent most of that first visit deciphering the rules. First, the festival is only for industry professionals and the media. It's not open to the larger public. Second, there is a strict colour-coded caste system—some badges allow more access than others. The most coveted badge for a journalist is the white one, which allows entry into screenings, press conferences and photocalls. The white badge is the Holy Grail and the festival's press department confers it when they deem you and your coverage deserving of it. How this is ascertained, no one knows. To get there, you must first jump through the hoops of yellow, blue, pink and pink-with-yellow-dot badges.

I think I started with a blue (described in a *Hollywood Reporter* article as 'the working-class badge' as opposed to the 'middle-class pink' and the 'landed-gentry white'). There were hardly any Indians at the festival then. I recall seeing only officials from the information and broadcasting ministry and filmmakers Shaji Karun and Murali Nair, whose films *Vanaprastham* and *Marana Simhasanam* were showing as part of the Un Certain Regard section. The National Film Development Corporation (NFDC) had a stall in the market, which is set up in the basement of the Palais des Festivals and where buyers and sellers conduct brisk business. Officials were trying to sell films like *Ambedkar* and *Janmadinam* but the neighbouring porno corridor was providing tough competition—starlets in skimpy clothing strutted up and down while titles like *Hard Knockers* were traded. Fortuitously, 1999 proved to be a big year for India—*Marana Simhasanam* won the Palme d'Or (given for best first film). It was the first Indian win at Cannes since Mira Nair's *Salaam Bombay!* eleven years earlier. It was exhilarating to see an Indian film take a top prize, and I understood then the prestige and power of the festival and why it exerts such a hold on the film industry globally.

In 2008, I was invited to be on the jury of Un Certain Regard, a prestigious sidebar to the main competition. The jury was headed by German filmmaker Fatih Akin. I was the only representative of India in the official programme—no Indian films had been selected. It was an enriching experience to watch films together and then argue passionately about which was better. That red carpet was also unforgettable—mostly because I walked with the entire jury, and a minder shadowed us the whole time, instructing us on which side to look so that photographers could get better photos. The micromanagement was impressive.

By this time, I had switched from print to television journalism. I was covering the festival for the national English-language news channel NDTV 24x7. Between jury duty and reporting duty, there was little time for food or sleep. Not surprisingly, midway through the festival, I fainted, in the Grand Theatre Lumiere, wearing a beautiful Abu Jani–Sandeep Khosla outfit, right after the screening of Steven Spielberg's *Indiana Jones and the Kingdom of the Crystal Skull* (causing my perplexed husband to remark, 'the film wasn't that bad'). The paramedics were called in. The problem was, I still had to do one last piece-to-camera for our television show. I eventually did it sitting in a wheelchair, which was hidden under my voluminous *anarkali* suit. There was something darkly funny and decidedly Cannes about the scene.

Over the years, the festival has become even more frenetic. Social media has added an urgency, so responses to films must be immediate. Along with print and digital coverage, we also need to constantly feed Twitter, Facebook and Instagram. All the while looking chic—Cannes demands a certain dress code. Even if no one is taking your photograph, you can't let the festival's fashion quotient down. The red carpet, of course, demands formals (a colleague was stopped for wearing jeans).

But even outside of it, there is an unsaid pressure to dress nicely, which I've never experienced at any other festival. The setting—the azure Mediterranean Sea and the row of expensive shops and hotels that line the main street, called La Croisette—demands that you also upgrade your style.

But what anchors Cannes and keeps us all going back, despite the ornery locals and the ridiculous prices, is the cinema. Every year, the festival premieres films that set the global palate and reveal something of the current zeitgeist. Artists are discovered here and reputations burnished. There might be controversy and debate, but the noise is fuelled by a furious love of film. Everyone who arrives at Cannes in mid-May has cinema in their bloodstream.

One of my lasting Cannes memories is of meeting the Pulitzer Prize-winning film critic Roger Ebert. Among critics of a certain generation, Ebert is the gold standard. His voice—erudite without being esoteric—shaped generations of film viewers and filmmakers too. He was a film critic for the *Chicago Sun-Times* from 1967 until his death in 2013. One of my favourite Ebert quotes is: 'Of all the arts, movies are the most powerful aid to empathy, and good ones make us into better people.' But it wasn't just his words that made me a devotee. It was his unmatched passion for movies, which continued even after he was diagnosed with cancer of the thyroid and salivary glands in 2002. Four years later, his lower jaw had to be removed and he lost the ability to speak. But he transformed himself into a formidable figure online, continuing to review and opine about the movies.

We met on Twitter. I was one of his thousands of followers but he followed me back because he said he was interested in Indian cinema and he liked that I wrote, despite the restrictive character count, full sentences with punctuation. We decided to meet in Cannes in the lobby of Hotel Splendid where he was staying. He communicated via written notes. We chatted about Bollywood, the festival and the films we had seen. He was warm and witty. Ebert had been attending Cannes since 1972—naturally there were many stories to exchange.

That meeting cemented in me an enduring love for Cannes. It will always be, to me, a movie circus where magic happens.

Acknowledgements

This book is not pandemic-induced. In February 2020, one month before life as we knew it changed, my editor Milee Ashwarya and I met in a New Delhi hotel and brainstormed over jasmine tea. The title—*A Place in My Heart*—was decided then. I want to thank her for persuading me to divert my energies from the instant gratification of digital journalism, and commit to the long-distance run of a book. Thank you to Zara Murao for dotting the i's and crossing the t's with such great care. Thank you to my family—Vinod, Agni, Zuni, KP—for the love and laughter and endless games of ludo that got us through multiple lockdowns. And to all the lovers of cinema who have read and watched my work—thank you for your support and faith. It has enabled me to do what I love for more than twenty-five years. It's been a privilege to share my passion with you.

References

- '16 Famous Bollywood Songs You Wouldn't Believe Were Copied From The West', *IndiaTimes*, 10 July 2015, https://www.indiatimes.com/entertainment/16-famous-bollywood-songs-you-wouldnt-believe-were-copied-from-the-west-234526.html.
- Brody, Richard, 'Does the Cinema Need Short Films?', *New Yorker*, 18 March 2014, https://www.newyorker.com/culture/richard-brody/does-the-cinema-need-short-films.
- Corliss, Richard, 'All-TIME 100 Movies', *Time*, 14 January 2010, https://entertainment.time.com/2005/02/12/all-time-100-movies/slide/nayakan-1987/.
- Digital, India Today, 'One-Man Industry (May 1-15, 1980)', *India Today*, 10 March 2010, https://www.indiatoday.in/magazine/30-years-ago-on-india-today/story/20100308-one-man-industry-may-1-15-1980-742197-2010-02-26.
- Jha, Lata. 'Sholay, 40 Years on: Remembering Minerva Theatre', *Mint*, 12 August 2015, https://www.livemint.

com/Consumer/hRPf7h8ebJyNXrwJQ5q2dM/Sholay-40-years-on-Remembering-Minerva.html.

- PTI, 'Delhi MMS Scandal Inspires Dibakar's Love, Sex Aur Dhoka', *India Today*, 29 December 2009, https://www.indiatoday.in/movies/bollywood/story/delhi-mms-scandal-inspires-dibakars-love-sex-aur-dhoka-63954-2009-12-29.
- 'Classics Revisited: Why Sholay Is a Cult Classic', Rediff.com, https://www.rediff.com/movies/2002/aug/09dinesh.htm.
- 'Saif Ali Khan: I Had No Idea What Kangana Was Saying on Koffee With Karan, I Was Surprised', Entertainment News by Zoom TV, https://www.zoomtventertainment.com/celebrity/article/saif-ali-khan-i-had-no-idea-what-kangana-was-saying-on-koffee-with-karan-i-was-surprised/615122.
- 'Sholay, the Beginning,', *Open*, 30 May 2019, https://openthemagazine.com/essays/arts-letters/sholay-the-beginning/.
- 'Sippys to Woo Indians with Sholay Cafe, Merchandise,' *Economic Times*, https://economictimes.indiatimes.com/industry/media/entertainment/sippys-to-woo-indians-with-sholay-cafe-merchandise/articleshow/27199820.cms?from=mdr.